CREDO: Personal Testimonies of Faith

Quinn was born in County Meath. He began his career as a teacher, but later became a radio producer and much-loved broadcaster with RTÉ. He has won many prestigious awards for his radio work. He is the author of *Goodnight Ballivor, I'll Sleep in Trim* (2008), which was also the subject of a TG4 documentary; *The Curious Mind: Twenty-Five Years of John Quinn Radio Programmes* (2009); *Letters to Olive: Sea of Love, Sea of Loss, Seed of Love, Seed of Life* (2011) and *Moments* (2011), all published by Veritas.

CREDO

PERSONAL TESTIMONIES OF FAITH

COMPILED AND EDITED BY
JOHN QUINN

VERITAS

Published 2014 by
Veritas Publications
7–8 Lower Abbey Street
Dublin 1, Ireland
publications@veritas.ie
www.veritas.ie

ISBN 978 1 84730 559 6

10 9 8 7 6 5 4 3 2 1

Extracts from 'The Great Hunger', 'Ploughman' and 'The Long Garden' by Patrick
Kavanagh are reprinted from *Collected Poems*, edited by Antoinette Quinn (Allen
Lane, 2004), by kind permission of the Trustees of the Estate of the late Katherine
B. Kavanagh, through the Jonathan Williams Literary Agency. 'The Club' by
Micheal Coady reprinted by kind permission of the author and The Gallery Press,
Loughcrew, Oldcastle, County Meath, Ireland, from *All Souls* (1997).

A catalogue record for this book is available from the British Library.

Designed by Heather Costello, Veritas Publications
Printed by W&G Baird Ltd, Antrim

The views and opinions expressed in this book are those of the individual
interviewees and do not necessarily reflect the views or opinions of the editor or
the publisher.

*Veritas books are printed on paper made from the wood pulp of managed forests. For
every tree felled, at least one tree is planted, thereby renewing natural resources.*

To my parents, Hugh Quinn and Brigid Ryan,
who believed and passed on that belief.

CONTENTS

INTRODUCTION

This book is the outcome of a series of interviews I conducted with twenty individuals during 2013. The interviews sought to elicit personal testimonies of faith from each of the interviewees – how they perceive the God they believe in, what is the source of that belief, what has nourished that belief and doubts they have encountered. The interviews further explored prayer and practice in the contributors' lives, how they cope with mystery, their views on the afterlife and the role of faith mentors in their lives.

I am deeply grateful to the participants for their openness, honesty and generosity in stating their religious beliefs. It is no easy thing, as I discovered, to subject oneself to such a personal and revealing interview and I am further in their debt on that account. I was so impressed, that I subjected myself to the same interview. The reader can judge the outcome of that self-interview in the final chapter of the book (page 169).

It is important to stress that the contributions to this book are testimonies of a particular kind. They are the spontaneous outcomes of one-to-one interviews. Were they considered and studied essays on the same topic, they would probably constitute a very different book, but not necessarily a more interesting one. There is, I contend, a freshness and an immediacy in the spontaneous that the considered essay can fail to capture. Added to that, the diversity of backgrounds and disciplines represented in the contributions will, I hope, add to the richness and overall attraction of this book.

John Quinn
March 2014

HARRY BOHAN

Harry Bohan has been a priest in the diocese of Killaloe for over fifty years. He is a pioneer in the areas of rural housing and community development in his native County Clare and is founder and director of the Céifin Institute, a think tank for values-led change. He is a hurling enthusiast and former manager of the Clare hurling team. His autobiography, Swimming Upstream, *was published in 2013.*

The God I believe in is the God I was brought up with and grew up with at home and in school in County Clare. He permeated all of life and accompanied us through the day. We talked to him all day – in the morning when we got up, during the day through the Angelus, in the evening at the rosary and last thing at night. He was present in our lives in all kinds of ways. At the weekend we gathered as a community to be in his presence. When anything sad happened – if, for example, a calf died – we were told it was the will of God. We coped with life by accepting the will of God.

My parents were hardworking and God-fearing people. My father was a garda and my mother ran our pub in Feakle and looked after her four children, for whom both parents made many sacrifices. Prayer, especially the rosary, and attendance at Mass and evening devotions, were built into the routine and structure of family and community life. In a small village like Feakle you were reared by the community almost as much as by your parents. I was lucky to live beside Paddy and Nellie Loughnane, who had a shop and a farm. They had no children and 'adopted' me from a young age. They would bring me to hurling matches and I would spend time with them on their farm. They were very loving people and I grew to love them greatly.

At school we learned the story of Jesus, his humble birth of a humble woman. The story stayed with me strongly all through my childhood. From an early age it struck me that the world was in a bad way for God to have sent his son to redeem us. All the previous prophets and leaders seemed to have failed. God was depicted in sacred pictures as a severe-looking man with a beard, but he became real to me through his son, Jesus. The Father in Heaven to whom I would eventually return was a vague and distant figure, but the God that meant a lot to me was Jesus. Saint Thomas Aquinas has said that the thing we know most about God is how little we know about him. For all that, I rejoiced every Christmas when we celebrated his coming into the world, and celebrated every Easter when he triumphed over death and opened the way to heaven for us. And the Last Supper always impacted on me because it reminded me of breaking from the comforts of home to return to boarding school. Overall though, it was a faith very much based on fear. The emphasis on sin and the need for regular confession (particularly as driven home at the annual mission) was unhealthy in retrospect.

Although we lived less than twenty miles from Ennis, I was sent as a boarder to St Flannan's College in that town. Boarding school was no picnic. I always hated going back there for a new term. Discipline was severe. There were priests there who beat us, even drew blood from our hands. I began to ask serious questions about the God they preached. St Flannan's was also a junior diocesan college but nothing I experienced there pointed me towards a vocation. Hunger, cold and discipline made life hard. The one real escape was hurling. In those times people believed that a priest had exceptional powers and were generally afraid of him. There was the anecdote of the priest who instructed a boy to hold his horse for him. When the boy refused, the priest threatened to stick him to the ground. Whereupon the boy said, 'If you are that powerful, why don't you stick the horse to the ground?'

For all that, I was inspired by two local men, Kevin Hogan and Tim Touhy, who joined the priesthood as I was growing up. They were very much of the people they served. I admired them and wanted to be like them. Vocations were 'in the air' then. Joining the priesthood would rank highly among the life choices young men would consider. I remember as a child playing 'Mass' in our kitchen, and the play became reality for me when I left St Flannan's for Maynooth in the late 1950s.

It was in Maynooth that I became involved in the world of sociology; that the real God, as opposed to the God of fear, came alive to me. This was the man who walked among the poor and the marginalised of this world and who raised up the humble. He pulled down those who abused power and he spent much time in prayer. When he was here on earth he asked his disciples, 'Who do people say I am?' I put that question a lot to myself in Maynooth. Who was Jesus? What did he mean to me? How can I follow what Jesus stood for? Ever since then I have come to realise that it was the person of Jesus who kept me in a relationship with God – the compassionate and healing Jesus, the Jesus who spoke out against hypocrisy and the abuse of power, the Jesus who took time out to reflect and pray and be with the Father. He is, in his own words, 'The Way, the Truth and the Life'. Following him is not about institutions or hierarchies, but about being with people, walking their difficult journeys, listening to them, identifying their needs and responding to those needs.

So it is through my parish duties that I find God; in the celebration of the Eucharist, which has always been a huge part of my life; in the classrooms of our schools as the children prepare for the sacraments. We have six brilliant young teachers doing that this year and the way they are preparing the children is truly amazing. We need the parents too. The three most important institutions in the parish are family, school and community. All three must be involved in preparing the children. I don't accept statements like, 'We only see the parents on First Communion or Confirmation day.' Parents have a huge role in transferring Christian values – telling the truth, showing courage, knowing right from wrong, being secure in our own skins. That is the power of Christianity. Likewise, I find God in bringing the Eucharist to old people in their homes – beautiful people who have coped with all the difficulties of life and lived their faith.

I am constantly searching for this God and for how best I can connect with him, find out what his message is for real people in the real world. I read a lot and reflect on what I read. I go back over a particular paragraph and ask, 'What is this saying? What does it mean for me?' Just recently, I read a book, *Beyond Prozac*, in which the author, Terry Lynch, states that 'According to the World Health Organization, depression will be the world's most pervasive serious illness by 2020. Currently, depression affects 340 million people.'[1] This has implications for the Church as much as for health systems. We need a new model of Church where priests like me need to move to a new kind of leadership, one of service rather than of authority.

Faith for me is a gift, but in the same way that Pope John Paul II said that the Eucharist is a gift and needs to be nourished, so faith also needs to be nourished through prayer. I still pray at the ritual times of my youth – morning, evening, night – and have remained faithful to my breviary reading over the years. Prayer can take many forms, of course. We are encouraged towards contemplative prayer. I am not great at it but I like to dwell on nature – mountains, lakes, trees – and consider the supernature that put it all there. It deepens my faith in him and my connection with him. We are encouraged to meditate on a piece of scripture – something I struggle with at times. The Mass is extremely significant for me as a priest. It is the core of my pastoral work so I take time before Mass to reflect on the readings. What is the Lord saying to us today and how does it connect to our daily lives? I talk to the congregation about that every morning. Over time I have come to believe that it is as important to break the word as it is to break bread.

---

1. Terry Lynch, *Beyond Prozac: Healing Mental Distress* (Ross-on-Wye: PCCS Books, 2004), p. 101.

As a young priest I was asked by Dr Thomas Morris, the Archbishop of Cashel and Emly, to give retreats for priests, and I have been doing that for years, covering most of the dioceses in Ireland. The preparation for these retreats and the need to constantly refresh my talks and reflections have helped to deepen my own faith. For most people the Sunday Eucharist is their closest connection with God, so it behoves me as a priest to make that celebration and my homily as relevant and meaningful as I can. I am heartened by the emergence of liturgy groups – mostly comprising women – who show wonderful creativity and talent in developing fresh and appealing liturgies for our community at various times of the year.

I recognise that there has been a lot of disillusionment with religion and its practice in recent years. There are people who drifted away because they saw the abuse that was going on in the Church. Others were genuinely disgusted and walked away. All of us who have accepted responsibility to connect the Christian message to life are challenged by this. Remember that people walked away from Jesus too, and he asked his disciples, 'Will you also go?' A lot of people are searching for a meaning to life and they will respond if the message is real and it makes sense to them. I know a man who has drifted away from the Church but he still comes to the community gathering on Sunday, to meet the Lord and thank him.

There is a new language needed. Very often it is too 'churchy' and doesn't make sense to people. We hardly ever use words like 'faith' or going to 'Mass' in Sixmilebridge. We talk about the 'gathering'. We gather as a community to hear Christ's message, to witness the bread and wine become the body and blood of Christ and to celebrate the fact that we are a community. For the past five years we have gathered in various locations – on a farm, in the mart, in a housing estate, at the railway station, in the cemetery – to celebrate the weekend Eucharist during the summer months. The community prepares for and organises the whole event which culminates in music, song and food. It is not so much about getting people back to the Church as getting the Church out to the people and connecting with them. And it works. I am heartened to hear Pope Francis plead for a Church and a priesthood that will touch people's lives and shape their environment. That's what the Sixmilebridge gatherings are attempting to do.

Mystery is a part of faith. The resurrection was always a big mystery for me. I went through a period of serious doubt about the afterlife. I remember a Mayo man saying to me in Birmingham, 'I don't believe in the afterlife, but I believe in Christianity because without it there would be no order in the world.' That made sense to me then but everything changed when my father died suddenly at Sunday Mass. For some reason it turned me to believing in an afterlife. Later I was with my mother when she died and I felt her soul had moved to another place. As John B. Keane said to me, 'If there weren't an afterlife, where would your parents be?' For myself I have no idea how God and I will meet. I love to hear people say, 'He'll welcome you', but I haven't a clue. We'll see what happens!

My faith mentors are those who have encouraged or inspired me over the years. Jimmy Doherty was my spiritual director in Maynooth. I had thoughts of leaving at one stage but he kept me on the right path. Michael Harty was my dean in Maynooth and later my bishop. He was very interested in community development and influenced me greatly in that area. He was a great leader and a wise and caring man. His successor, Willie Walsh, has been a great example to me. A very humble man who prays a lot and lives the faith. A very brave man whose motto *Cineáltas Chríost* ('the kindness of Christ') was exemplified in his care for the marginalised, especially the Travellers. And a very honest man who never shirked issues such as child abuse, the role of women in the Church and the Church's attitude to gay people. I was a great fan of the late Cardinal Martini of

Milan. A wonderfully open-minded man who could read the signs of the times and act accordingly. He famously said that the Church is two hundred years behind the times. For him it was all about connecting Christ's word to the real lives of people. He was an amazing man, equally adept as a scholar and a pastor. Julius Nyerere, the Tanzanian leader, came here to study the co-operative movement and impressed me greatly. He was a man of deep faith and a daily Massgoer. My own parents of course provided a faith-filled home, but generally those who influenced me were the doers and the prophets, the people who lived the faith more than praying. Emma Spence summed it up when she spoke at the funeral service of her father and brothers who died in a tragic farm accident: 'They didn't talk God. They did God.'

The journey we walk now is Christ's journey. It is a challenge and not a time to be going through the motions. It was unhealthy when it was all about power and everybody was 'believing'. I have confidence in my belief now only because in recent years I've dug deeper in my relationship with Jesus. I am not going to apologise for who I am and what I stand for. Rather I will nourish my belief through prayer and reflection. Barack Obama was recently re-elected the most powerful man in the world. For how long will he be remembered? Two thousand years on we are still remembering Jesus Christ, and now in a period of crisis we are digging ever deeper to find connection with the person of Jesus.

SEÁN BOYLAN

Seán Boylan is a herbalist who continues a family tradition stretching over many generations in his native Dunboyne, Co. Meath. Former long-serving manager of the Meath Gaelic football team, he brought much success to the county, including four All-Ireland titles. His autobiography The Will to Win, *co-written with John Quinn, was published in 2006.*

I have a very simple faith: a belief in a God that provides for us and loves us and asks us in return to love him and love our neighbour. I derive great solace and comfort from that faith. It has been a huge influence all through my life. I can never remember a time when I did not want to believe. It was part of the culture I grew up in and the home that shaped me, but within that home there was always an extraordinary tolerance of other persuasions and other values.

My father was a herbalist and a soldier. A knowledge of the healing power of herbs has been in our family for many generations. I carry on that tradition today in my clinic in Dunboyne, Co. Meath. My father was a member of the Irish Volunteers during the Easter Rising and the subsequent War of Independence. He supported Michael Collins and the pro-Treaty side in the Civil War. In 1919 he was seriously wounded in an accidental explosion and at one stage was given a year to live. But he lived on for another fifty years, due in no small part to the heroic care of my mother who bathed and dressed his arms and legs daily over that period. They were a hardworking, devoted couple whose ethos in life was 'Mind the sick, bury the dead, pray for those in need, help wherever you can and don't make an exhibition of it'! It was in that ethos I grew up.

The practice of religion was central to our lives. I became an altar boy, having made a successful pitch for the job to the parish priest one Christmas Eve. Our year was marked by a cycle of rituals, most of them related to religious practice. On St Patrick's Day we would visit my father's family in Dublin, go to Mass in Arran Quay and then watch the parade. At Halloween, apples were brought from our orchards to the Capuchin Friary in Church Street for distribution to the poor. In November we did the rounds of city churches – St Peter's in Phibsboro, Gardiner Street, Clarendon Street, Whitefriar Street – with our List of the Dead.

Little wonder then that my main ambition from a young age was to be a priest. I was particularly interested in the Cistercian Order. Childhood visits to Mount Melleray and Roscrea left a lasting impression. I was not overly pious but I felt I needed God in my life. Whatever talents I had were God-given and I felt I had to pay for those talents in the service of God. I struggled with that right through my twenties and thirties, despite having a normal social life. I discussed my problem with an uncle of mine, Fr Willie Quinn, and his wise advice was, 'Even though it is a great honour and privilege to be a priest, sometimes you can do better work in the world, but it never settles until you get peace of mind with the decision yourself.' The moment of revelation came many years later.

I was treating a young woman in Northern Ireland for persistent skin infections. I had been to see her over fifty times in all. On one particular weekend she was very poorly indeed. I visited her on Thursday, came home and worked all day Friday before returning to see her again on Friday night. I was so concerned about her that I went back again on Saturday evening. Thankfully she finally turned the corner that night and made a full recovery. I remember that morning so vividly. It was a beautiful spring Sunday, and the fields were glistening with frost as I headed for home. On the way I stopped at the Cistercian monastery at Collon, Co. Louth, for Mass. I met one of the monks. His name was Giolla Chríost (although he came from Kansas). We said we would pray for each other. I went into the chapel and there it became clear to me at last: I needed God alright, but in the world, not in an enclosed order. I was the only boy in a family of six and I would be needed at home to continue the family tradition of herbalism.

I left Warrenstown Agricultural College to help, and learn from, my father. It was the best decision I ever made. My father was over half a century older than me and we would never have kicked a ball together as father and son might normally do, but we had ten years together during which I learned from him the great wisdom he had absorbed from previous generations. I would serve God best by employing that wisdom in the care and healing of others.

My sense of God is that he is present everywhere, in everything. I walk through my fields and see little plants like the ox-eye daisy, and my favourite, parsley piert. I wonder at what they can do in the treatment of the sick and I see God in them. I feel his presence all about me. At times it can be very, very strong, like a kind of energy. There is a graveyard down the road in Loughsallagh, where my people are buried. I can feel his energy particularly there. The world is full of the wonders of nature, which in turn reflect the greatness of God. I can only marvel at how seeds will die in the ground to provide new growth. In South America there is a desert which flowers only every ten years. Why? How? Look at the awesome power of the winds and oceans. When the tsunami hit Thailand, how did the elephants sense its coming and run before it arrived? The mystery and power of God is all about us. For me, it is captured so powerfully in Joseph Mary Plunkett's poem 'I See His Blood Upon the Rose'.

> I see his blood upon the rose
> And in the stars, the glory of his eyes,
> His body gleams amid eternal snows,
> His tears fall from the skies.

I see his face in every flower;
The thunder and the singing of the birds
Are but his voice – and carven by his power
Rocks are his written words.

All pathways by his feet are worn,
His strong heart stirs the ever-beating sea,
His crown of thorns is twined with every thorn,
His cross is every tree.[1]

Extraordinary as nature is, what of the human being, the miracle of life that happens every time a child is born? Tina and I have been blessed with that miracle six times. Many years ago, a nun from the USA gave me a present of a book in gratitude for my treatment of her condition. It was entitled *Fearfully And Wonderfully Made*, a collaboration between Philip Yancey, a writer, and Paul Brand, an orthopaedic surgeon, on the miracle that is the human body.[2] The title comes from Psalm 139, verses 13-14: 'You created my inmost being; You knit me together in my mother's womb. I praise You because I am fearfully and wonderfully made.' Doctor Brand spent a lifetime treating leprosy and studying and observing the human body. He wrote:

I have come to realise that every patient of mine, every newborn baby in every cell of its body, has a basic knowledge of how to survive and how to heal, that exceeds anything I shall ever know. That knowledge is the gift of God, who has made our bodies more perfectly than we could ever have devised.

---

1. Joseph Mary Plunkett, 'I See His Blood Upon the Rose,' *The Oxford Book of English Mystical Verse*, D. H. S. Nicholson and A. H. E. Lee, eds. (Oxford: The Clarendon Press, 1917), p. 560.

2. Philip Yancey and Paul Brand, *Fearfully and Wonderfully Made* (Grand Rapids, MI: Zondervan Publishing House, 1980).

That book became my bible in the way it pays tribute to the miracle of the human body as a representation of God's work. For example, if you look at our skin – something we might take for granted – and then you stop and think of what it does: it encases the entire body; it stretches, breathes, blushes, pales, waterproofs, perspires, tingles, pains, itches, glows, glistens, and acts as a frontline defence against the hordes of bacteria that relentlessly attack the human body. What a miracle! That book reminds me especially of the greatest healer of all, Jesus Christ.

The other aspect of Paul Brand's story that resonates with me is his concept of service. When he looks back on his life, it's not the awards he won or the amazing holidays he had that bring him pleasure. Rather it is his work in the service of others, particularly lepers, in primitive conditions and with basic equipment. Our culture extols self-fulfilment and self-advancement, but according to Christ, it is only in losing my life that I will find it. I must see God in the people who come to me and only by committing myself to others through loyalty to him will I find my true reason for being. Each of us has different gifts but no one is born with all the knowledge. One of the greatest gifts is listening. There was a conference recently in New York where a famous diagnostician spoke about all the aids we have – tests, scans, imaging – to help us find what is wrong. We see an average of four and a half patients an hour, he said, yet we don't realise the greatest evidence we have is sitting in front of us. If we talk, ask the right questions and listen, we will get most of the answers we seek. Tests won't tell you what makes someone angry or happy, what makes them cry or smile. Someone has to empower that person by listening.

I wouldn't be the most organised person, religion-wise, but prayer is an important part of my life. If I'm going somewhere, or am asked to speak at a function, I begin with a prayer – often the Memorare (my favourite prayer) or the Serenity Prayer. The rosary beads travel everywhere with me too. I pray to God for direction in my work; not in the sense of a blind faith but for a better understanding of what I am doing. When I began managing the Meath football team, I just happened to tell the lads at our first training session that there was Mass after our training session. 'Do we have to go?' they asked. 'No, I'm just telling you it's on.' But they went, and it became a sort of ritual before every championship match. It was a lovely thing to see. For my part, I would pray for guidance, never for victory, because God is on both sides. Just be thankful for the talents we have and do the best we can with them. If our best is not good enough, it doesn't mean we are failures.

I like ritual. The first time I was in the Vatican, I thought it was the most pagan place ever – full of people jostling to be photographed beside the *Pietà* and so on! I wanted to run out of the place but once the ceremonies [for the beatification of Oliver Plunkett] began, it was a totally different place.

Some years ago our business was in severe trouble due to an abortive herb contract. In a dream one night I learned that I had to go to Lourdes. By chance at a funeral I met four army chaplains who wanted me to accompany them to Lourdes. I went in 1982, and despite a fear of water I went into the baths. When I came out I noticed a statement in seven languages: 'Wash your face and pray to God to cleanse your heart'. That message has stayed with me ever since. And we did survive the financial crisis. The family motto is *Dominus providebit*, 'The Lord will provide'.

One of my great faith mentors is the Benedictine monk, Laurence Freeman. I met him at a retreat in Glenstal Abbey and had long discussions with him. We became soulmates. He rang me when my sister Frances died and when I was about to undergo surgery for a tumour. I had read a lot of Thomas Merton's work and was delighted when Laurence came to Dublin with Abbe Le Care, who was the friend and mentor of Merton. Some things are just meant to happen! Laurence is very involved with the Christian Meditation Movement and he taught me to welcome stillness – never to be afraid to open my mind and in turn my heart. That energises me greatly.

Of course I have had doubts and falterings in my faith life. Sometimes we wonder where is God in the midst of suffering. My sister had an aneurysm and is totally paralysed. I asked her husband and children if they ever despaired. They thought about it and said no, not really. Such amazing courage is hard to rationalise, but I suppose in times of trial we pray together in a lifeboat situation. There is a plaque outside my office which says 'Bidden or not bidden, God is present'. I was at a function in Pieta House [the suicide and self-harm crisis centre] yesterday and was asked to say a few words. I didn't know where to start or finish. I thought of Spike Milligan, who made us all laugh despite his manic depression. His daughter once asked him, where does the dark go when you turn on the light? For people dealing with suicide, it is the opposite question: what happens when the light goes out and they are in the dark? At times like that you can only hand things over to your Maker and hope for his guidance.

Overall, my faith has stood me well but I went through a valley period when a very good priest friend of mine was blackened by his own church authorities. Untruths were told about him and his character was continually sullied over a period of two years. I found it incredibly offensive and it certainly rocked my faith. The truth eventually came out but no one in authority had the courage to admit they were wrong. It affected the faith of his flock – a number never went back to the Church. It was a very dark episode, but difficult though it was, I never stopped believing. I was following my own father's way. His name was read off the altar in denunciation after the 1916 Rising but it never stopped him going to Mass and he never fell out with the priest. 'I'll lose my soul for no man, priest or otherwise,' he declared.

I don't particularly look forward to death. I had a near-death experience when I almost drowned in a swimming pool and, believe me, it was not pleasant. I feel I have an awful lot of things to do yet – not for myself, but for others. I don't feel things are right just yet. I believe in an afterlife, although I have no idea what form it will take – and I am not in any hurry to find out! I have no doubt but that my parents are guiding me now. There is such energy about – it can't all be due to physics. The Holy Spirit and the holy souls are all around us. And the outstretched hands of the Lord will be there to welcome us. The afterlife will be good, and as the Lord said, 'In my father's house are many rooms.' There are many ways of knowing God. Fanaticism – my way or no way – is a very dangerous thing. That's not the way it is. Our Maker is above that.

JOAN CHITTISTER

Joan Chittister is an American-born Benedictine nun who lives in Erie, Pennsylvania. She is an international speaker and leader for peace and justice, and executive director of Benetvision, a Resource and Research Centre for Contemporary Spirituality. A prolific author, her recent books include Happiness *(2011),* Following the Path: The Search for Passion, Purpose and Joy *(2012),* Art of Life *(2012),* The Sacred In-Between *(2013),* The Way of the Cross *(2013) and* A Passion for Life *(2013).*

This is a crossover point in time, very similar to that Galileo moment in history when he changed our conception of the world. Galileo was condemned because his science was in contradiction to the established theology. Science up to that time affirmed what they thought they knew, but it now contradicted what they were sure they knew. We are right back at that moment in time again, only now we call it evolution. Talk of Big Bangs and a hundred thousand universes turns everything you have learned upside down – but does it attack faith? I argue that I have got to the point in studying this science very carefully where I am at a marvellous spiritual moment, in which evolution is in a sense my spiritual director. God, to me, is no longer an old man on a cloud with a stopwatch. All of those old images of God – the Gotcha God who says 'I made you, you tripped, gotcha, it's over', or the God that will make the red light turn green before I get to the corner – are sweet myths, some of them even terrifying. But what science gives me now is this picture of the God of Life that has welcomed us into that life as co-creators. 'Here's your world,' he is saying. 'No, I haven't answered everything. No, I haven't solved everything. I have given it to you and I want you to make of it the best you can and I will be with you as you go.'

All of a sudden everything that real theologians and mystics have taught us above those childhood myths becomes startlingly real to me. God is Emmanuel. God is God-with-us. When Moses asks 'Who are you?' the answer doesn't come just 'I Am Who Am'. If you know Hebrew, you go all the way down to the last line: 'I am with you'. I believe now in this God who companions us as – like all of evolution – we stumble, we fall, we get up, we go on. Failure is built into the process. There is nothing to be afraid of. We are working our way to our best selves and God is with us as we do it. Hierarchy is not built into that process. All of life is of the same elements – popes, paupers, potentates, police – we are all there, working, failing, getting up. This awareness of God has given me a whole new sense of the fire and the light in scripture and in life.

My father died when I was three, leaving my mother a widow at twenty-one. It was a very difficult time, at the end of the Depression. My mother re-married a wonderful Presbyterian man, Dutch Chittister, who had never set foot in a church but taught me great spiritual values, especially that of truth. He had character, integrity and strength. I was therefore an ecumenist before it was a word, let alone a virtue. We moved to Erie after the war; to a very small apartment in a very poor area, but I treasure that experience. I learned about humanity and suffering. We were a forgotten but a strong community.

My father was totally against a Catholic education for me, but my mother insisted. I loved school at first with the Sisters of St Joseph, and later with the Benedictines. I wanted to be a nun from the age of three, when the sisters came to give Daddy's soul to the angels, who would then give it to God. I didn't have a model Catholic family background but, ironically, the mixed marriage broadened my sense of faith. It gave me a perspective of the world where diversity came in different people and different ways. I couldn't understand how the same God could condemn my Protestant grandmother and save my

Catholic grandmother, so at the age of eight I chose to believe that somebody was wrong. Later, as I delved into history and saw the politicisation of religion in the worst possible persecutional way, I knew there was enough wrong to go around.

I began to pay attention to the God of Scripture – the God who saved, who cared, who sent forth Jonah to convert a people he didn't like. Jonah was sent to Nineveh but instead went in the opposite direction, until he was thrown overboard, swallowed by the whale and eventually disgorged on the shore he was intended for. And then we have that beautiful sentence when the Lord says, 'Jonah, do you not know me after all this time? I am mercy upon mercy upon mercy.' These stories, and the Jesus story, shaped me and I just let the Gotcha God and all those other images fall away like scales from my eyes. Then, when evolution burst on the scene, God-with-us became my God.

I originally intended to join the wonderful Sisters of St Joseph, but when I went to high school and heard the Benedictines chanting their office, I just knew I would join them. I did so on my sixteenth birthday, despite their reluctance to accept an only child because mother would need me in later life. My mother insisted that she didn't want my life affected by hers, so I entered and began a formation that was totally liturgical, totally prayer and scripture-oriented. My father's reaction was terrible. It took him years to adjust. My parents visited the monastery once a month and he would sit for hours in the car waiting for my mother. Then, gradually, because the nuns refused to resist and ignore him, his heart turned and he eventually fell in love with them.

Within six weeks of entering, I contracted polio and spent four years in wheelchairs, iron lungs and braces, learning to walk again. I insisted on doing the same work everyone else did. The nuns never gave up on me and did the exercises with me every day until the nerves began to regenerate and I became functional again. In those days there was a theology of suffering – God wanted this for you for some reason. It had a place then but I don't believe in it now. I would say now that that was life, and life is what we go through to become the best living being we can be. For me also at that time my spiritual life was greatly developed, steeped as a Benedictine in scriptures and lectio, but also through reading the writings of the mystics. I blossomed in the whole spiritual tradition that enfolded me.

And yet, ten years later I wanted to leave the order! It was the 1960s, a period of great change. Within religious communities, prayer-life, habits and rules were changing. I am not an intuitive person, I need to study everything. Was I leaving religious life or was it leaving me? The more questions I asked, the more I realised that this way of life had a quality that no amount of schedules, rules or uniforms could provide. So I stayed, but I was glad that I had tested the idea of leaving in my own mind.

The monastery is a community which becomes your family. Benedictines keep a common table and live a common prayer life. We believe strongly that the function of our community is to be a stable presence in an area, a place where people come for refreshment and support. Hospitality is a major part of our life and there is never a penny charged. That is why writers like Hemingway, Greene, Alan Paton, Steinbeck – those who exposed the plight of the poor – had a great effect on me. I have long since left the realm of catechesis and Canon Law and I walked instead the road from Galilee to Jerusalem. Then this God of Evolution comes in, gives you the components of life in your world and says, 'Shape them. Fix them!'

I do not believe God makes people poor: we make people poor; our economic systems make people poor; our lack of Christian development makes people poor. I feel a great obligation to be part of the creative process, somehow or other. I am not saying everyone should work in a soup kitchen. I haven't served two cups of soup in my life, but my role as teacher, advocate, minister, enables the soup kitchens to exist, doors to be opened, people to be found. Poverty dispirited me for years. I thought of the years when I could have been sitting in a chapel or at a lakeside contemplating God in the sunset. I thought of the life values – security, progress, achievement – that I never gave myself to, until I suddenly realised that that wasn't where the fullness of faith life was for me. This God of Evolution was saying this world is yours to shape and create. That's why we are here, all of us.

Benedictines take a vow of stability. We live and die in the same monastery. We don't come in pyramids, with one superior at the top and little houses dotted all over the world where you can move around. We live rather in circles, so that the community you are in is the family that is your responsibility. We believe in stability of place, staying committed to the people of this place all your life. Our monastery is in Erie, Pennsylvania. Erie is one of the five Great Lakes. Thirty years ago it was 'dead' due to pollution. What happens to Lake Erie happens to my community, therefore it is my responsibility to the people of Erie to do what I can do to preserve that lake. So the Benedictines and four other groups sued the State over the pollution and won. That is a very clear manifestation of our vow of stability. We rise and fall with the character and circumstances of the place where we live. The people rub edges off you. You become a different person because of the people to whom you are committed.

As Benedictines we pray chorally three times a day with two separate lectio periods. It never changes. Even away from the community as I am now, I read from the breviary and so I am in rhythm with my community. Saint Benedict tells us very clearly to keep prayer brief, because the communal aspects of prayer are intended to oil and maintain private prayer, and that is where the contemplative dimension of Benedictine life comes in.

Since 1952 that prayerful life has been dripping into my soul like the Chinese water trick day after day, aloud and then in private reflection. For me a contemplative is a person who sees the world through the eyes of God, and when that has a scriptural basis it is clearly a desire to be immersed in the mind of God. It's not a matter of saying rosaries or visiting the Blessed Sacrament. In that immersion process you don't say a prayer, you become a prayer. In one of my books I describe prayer as 'the breath of the soul', simply because when your prayer is so substantial and so constant, it becomes part of the atmosphere around you, the lungs of your soul, as it were. Prayer in my life is now bigger than ever, clearer than ever and more constant and more important than ever.

Most of my faith mentors are the older sisters in our community; [they are] profoundly holy kind of women for whom prayer was clearly the foundation on which their lives stood. I talk to them and they quote scripture at me because it is for them a perfectly normal part of the conversation. It is the grist of their lives. In the rule of Benedict there are scriptural references in every chapter – if you believe this, then you will do that. Other great mentors were Dietrich Bonhoeffer, Dorothy Day and Thomas Merton, particularly the latter. I learned from them what the exigencies of scripture were, what their attitudes towards events were and why. I have always talked about melting into the mind of God because years ago I put down all definitions other than God as 'life'. That probably came as a result of reading Pierre Teilhard de Chardin in the 1960s; he didn't know what the afterlife was like but he talked of the stream of life.

I have great faith that life goes on in another form, but if not, it doesn't bother me. The Godlife has been here with me all my life. Someone has said, 'If there is a God there is nothing to worry about, and if there isn't a God there is nothing to worry about!' If this is the fullness, then that has been a great consciousness of the divine. I don't believe it is the fullness. When I was a little girl we were always told that at the end of time, life will return. Then the scientists tell us that in maybe four or five billion years everything will melt into one stream of life. For me, that's the end of time – we will all know God and life differently. I have no time for fancy images of heaven or of some sort of children's paradise. I believe that life will come to wholeness in the God who is life and that is enough for me. I see 'life' as the birth canal to the fullness of that life. I have a great feeling of God-with-us and I am not afraid.

If I could have walked with Jesus, I would love to have been present for the Sermon on the Mount, to hear him pronounce the eight beatitudes as the template of happiness. Most of all, though, I would love to have been with Jesus at his most unorthodox moments – for example, when he was confronted by the Canaanite woman: 'I don't even have anything to do with you.' 'If you are who you say you are, do something!'

Oh to have seen him walk with those women disciples, to realise the equality of all that! The image of woman that the Church gives me is not the image I get from Jesus. We have had two thousand years of patriarchal plutocracy and I just know that was not the will of Jesus for women. We were not created 'bone of my bone and flesh of my flesh' so that God could tease us by being useless. We need to have a discussion on what it means for a woman to also be a minister, a carrier of the Holy Spirit, a purveyor of wisdom, a means and an instrument of grace. We are gradually building a critical consciousness. In thirty or forty years' time this conversation won't be a trouble to anyone; it will simply be of the essence of thought in the western world.

When I look at the Church I find an institution that does not look to me like what Jesus meant in the gospels. For years that was disappointing to me to the point of disillusionment, but I am way beyond that now. I really believe that every day the Jesus story gets brighter and the institution gets dimmer. I believe what I was taught – that the Jesus who raised the dead, cured lepers and said, 'Go and do likewise', meant it. How can you be a Christian and do otherwise?

PAT CLARKE

Pat Clarke has been a member of the Spiritans (Holy Ghost Fathers) for almost fifty years. He was born in the Liberties of Dublin and lived later in County Kildare. He has spent most of his priestly life in Brazil, working with the poor in the favelas. The philosophy of his friend, the Brazilian educationist Paulo Freire, 'Travel with people, not in front or behind' has been a major influence in his life.

I grew up in the Liberties of Dublin in a traditional Irish Catholic family – rosary every night and Mass every Sunday, sometimes twice. My mother had originally been a Protestant but became a Catholic. She never pushed anything on us and was just a quiet, faithful, very humorous person who didn't talk about faith but lived it. There was no big show, no ostentation. I was the eldest of six children, which brought a certain responsibility. I was a bit of a loner at school and in my early teens I was attracted to the religious life. As a boy I would make little altars and was fascinated with the sacred. In my teens the idea of religious life just grew and of course, in the time that was in it, there were not many options for the product of a simple, poor Irish home.

I told my mother of my plan when I was about fourteen and I can still see the shock on her face. My father was less shocked and was keen for me to join the Oblates because a friend of his had done so, but I declined. The notion of service attracted me and I eventually met a lad who had been in a Holy Ghost seminary. He advised me to go there. I did, and have had no regrets ever since. I was a very applied, serious student. It wasn't a great education but there was a great sense of community; you belonged to something that was bigger than you. I went to a seminary in Britain and a novitiate in France. That was a liberating experience – embracing a new language, culture and environment and meeting people of different nationalities. In the middle of all this came Vatican II, which was new and exciting, giving you a sense of responsibility and allowing you to become a person rather than a number in an institution. I often wonder would I still be in the priesthood were it not for Vatican II. I was being questioned, shaken up, made to look seriously at how the Church could be the People of God rather than a big monolith.

I was ordained in 1965, so Vatican II came at the right time for me and I am grateful. There were rumours of being sent to Africa but instead I was sent to teach in a seminary in the Lake District, before pursuing further study in University College Dublin and Boston College. I met a man who was a Provincial in Brazil. He invited me to join him. I did and I never looked back. When I was there for a while I was so glad I hadn't gone to Africa. Here in the shanty towns of Brazil there was tremendous possibility, pastorally speaking. As a result of Vatican II, I was trying to be a learner. The great educationist Paulo Freire – who would subsequently influence me a lot – said, 'Every teacher is a learner and every learner is a teacher.' I thought that this, pastorally, was the right way to be.

On reflection, Europe and Africa were too structured, too monolithic for my liking. In the favelas there is a strong community structure, but you couldn't possibly impose a parish structure there. It just wouldn't work. As Freire said, you need to be a fly on the wall. Observe, listen and then see how you might contribute. Look at things at the people's pace and bring them with you. No authoritarian, big bang intervention. A bishop said recently to me, 'You've done all these projects – community centre, pastoral centre, centre of culture – but where's the church?' I said I thought that is what I had been doing all along. If it's not the people, what's the point of a building? Two years ago we did build a church and all the sacred work is decorated by the youth of the shanty town in the art school we have there.

My first visit to the favelas was a real culture shock! There are thousands of them in the city. I didn't know how to approach them but I immediately saw that these people have something we have thrown away: community. They have values and are not just to be pitied. Any time I am with them we have the greatest conversations and I am always sad leaving them. Freire gave us this tool of talking to people in terms they understand. So you analyse the words they use – pray, church, child, sewer, food, hunger, disease, etc. – and work within that. They will say 'We don't know anything, we are not educated', so you work on that. I would say, 'Would you like to gather to pray this evening?' and everyone squeezes into a small house because they are very religious people. We say the rosary while rats scuttle around, and the stench from the sewers is overpowering. You cannot shove things down their throats, otherwise you become an oppressor.

We continued to pray in different houses for a long time until I made a breakthrough (probably by joking about christening the rats!). Who made that table? This house? Everyone had a hand in it. The big question was how would they accept that I didn't know any more than them? Back to Freire again. You play a game; you invent a word they don't know. One–nil to you. Now they invent a word I don't know. One–all. And so on … 2–1, 2–2, 3–2, 3–3. So who knows more than anyone else here? No one! Breakthrough! So do you want to keep the rats and the stench? No! Can we do something? And don't tell me you don't know!

Out of that came the sewerage project, a sort of theology of sewers, from the ground up. It was a community experience, not someone who 'knew' coming along and saying, 'This is how you do it.' With the help of an engineer friend, we divided the whole area into fifty-two sections and the community got out their spades, hoes, bare hands. Over five years we completed the project. That for me is the way belief travels. It is a pilgrimage where you have many questions but you don't have a basic doubt that this is the road, because you are dealing with a God of surprises.

All of this experience would erode and explode the narrow channel I had grown up in. The ability to change is an amazing thing. Saint Teresa of Ávila was stuck until late in her life in a method of prayer that was no good to her. John Henry Newman said that to live is to change and to be perfect is to have changed often. When he was about to enter the Catholic Church, he was beleaguered by people who said, 'Don't do it! It will be a disaster!' He persisted. If you are going because it is a journey, that's not a disaster. It may have a disastrous history, but the journey as such isn't a disaster. The journey is the metaphor.

I did the Camino [de Santiago] walk in 1999. That was a tremendous inscape as well as a wonderful landscape; I was making the journey within as well as without. It was very deep and disturbing to be out there on the mountain alone, where you could roar out your grief or joy. I roared about injustices I had committed, people I had wronged. Stuff came up that I didn't even know was there. I met two Americans who had been married for forty-four years. They nearly divorced afterwards when they learned they didn't know each other at all! The Camino gives you self-knowledge and a sense of gratitude that the Lord is so tolerant, so merciful, so unconditionally accepting.

I like the Gospel of Luke because it is a gospel of mercy – the prodigal son, the lost sheep, etc. He travelled with Paul and saw the world as much bigger than simply the Jewish view of Matthew, for example. It's about being pure in heart: 'Blessed are the pure in heart for they shall see God.' I put that on my mother's gravestone because she was pure in heart, a child all her life. The Lord didn't say the kingdom shall belong to adults, but to children, so what have we done to our 'child'? If you have the child within, you are close to God.

Recovering that child within is a conversion experience. A moment of crisis is very often when it can happen. In Brazil we make these dolls out of bottle tops. A single bottle top would be trash. What makes it possible to look at it again and see that it is not just trash? The eye of a child. As Kavanagh says, 'In a crumb of bread the whole mystery is.'[1] That is the conversion point. The whole thing is in the first step, as with the sewers in our case. This is the gospel, in my view. This is the mustard seed, the lost sheep, the prodigal son. Imagination is hard work and often we are not prepared for that. Michelangelo spent a lot of time chipping away at the marble block before a foot appeared. We want the harvest but we don't want to sow the seed. With imagination you have got to believe, but you cannot believe on your own. As St Paul said, 'How can they know if no one goes to tell them?' There has to be someone who carries the news, a catalyst. The sense that everything good comes out of the base is heresy, because the base cannot be renewed unless something comes in. Basic biology tells you that the cell on its own goes nowhere.

Paulo Freire has been a huge influence on my life. We became good friends and I translated his last, and in my opinion finest, book, *Pedagogy of Freedom*. Some phrases from the core of his thinking include: 'We have to talk about the obvious'; 'Don't go in with a ready-made project'; 'Be a fly on the wall – listen!'; 'Travel with people, not in front or behind'; 'Every teacher is also a learner. Every learner is also a teacher'; 'Don't pretend that your story can imitate the story of someone else. Meet their story'.

Freire influenced, and was influenced by, Liberation Theology. You are not an indoctrinator, you are on a journey. That is the basic thing about the 'people of God' image. As a missionary, I see my role as trying to keep a community in a cohesive dynamic. There are many conflicts in a community and you become a reference point for dialogue, understanding, forgiveness. Basic communities have generated so much else, in terms of social awareness, in projects linked to the life of their faith. It really is a gospel of many dimensions.

---

1. Patrick Kavanagh, 'The Great Hunger', *Collected Poems*, Antoinette Quinn, ed. (London: Allen Lane, 2004), p. 72.

Dorothy Day is another great hero of mine, because she set out on a journey with many obstacles in front of her. She was a journalist who became a member of the Communist Party and a sort of anarchist. She was involved in a relationship and had a daughter, whom she had baptised to give the child the spiritual foundation she herself had lost. She embraced Catholicism and was converted and became a devout Catholic. A big turning point in her life was meeting Peter Maurin, a French immigrant of peasant background who was an amazing philosopher. He elaborated a project about life that inspired her greatly and together they founded the Catholic Worker Movement, which offered houses of hospitality in the cities and farms for communal living in rural areas. Their newspaper, *The Catholic Worker*, promoted Catholic social teaching. Dorothy was in and out of prison over protesting about the arms race and workers' conditions. She travelled the world preaching God's love and pacifism. Despite ill-health, she was so amazing in her consistency. Today there are over one hundred CWM communities all over the world. Her autobiography, *The Long Loneliness*, is an inspiring read.

Aquinas spoke of God as *summum bonum* – total good – and to me total good has to include beauty and the arts. I believe there is a fundamental link between faith and imagination. There is a wonderful Jesuit author, William F. Lynch, who has written about this. He talks of despair as an absence or a destruction of the imagination. One of the tragedies of our Church is the way the imagination has been neglected. We don't teach children catechism in isolation in Brazil. We do it through families and we employ theatre and art and story, and *then* the theoretical stuff hangs on that, but you always begin with the experience. The Irish people have such capacity for storytelling. Why has it not been incorporated in the liturgy? The child is being expelled again. The imagination is being marginalised. Faith as just a simple rational wanting to me is a dead thing. It's not part of my understanding of God. That is why the Brazil experience has meant so much to me.

Out of the faith/imagination thing came our centre for art and culture: a campus with five buildings – very simple buildings – illuminated with wine bottles of different colours, our 'stained glass'. This is for kids who live on top of each other, with no place to play, not a blade of grass anywhere. They go into the centre and are stunned. They do art, puppetry, sculpture, music, judo, karate, drumming, dance, ballet. Respect is imposed on them by the environment. This enables us to pass on teaching about life, wonder, story, art, faith. This is the challenge of the gospel – being there because you believe it and you never know what will happen. If the Lord wants this to survive, he will find a way. That's good enough for me. There is a Brazilian poet, Adélia Prado, whom I like very much. She is a very strong believer who continually revisits her faith. She says in one of her poems, 'Some things just are.'

Belief is a work in progress. If you are lucky, you get to a point where you feel secure even though you have many questions. I come back again to community. I see these people around me who have been massacred by life but there is never despair. I have never experienced one suicide in thirty-six years of living in the shanty town. These people can teach me so much about living. This is the journey – and for me there isn't any other show in town.

MICHAEL COADY

Michael Coady is a poet, writer and a former teacher who has lived and worked all his life in Carrick-on-Suir, Co. Tipperary. Much of his writing is influenced by his native place and its people. His publications include Oven Lane *(1987),* All Souls *(1998),* One Another *(2003) and* Going by Water *(2009). He is a member of Aosdána.*

In some ways, my belief surprises me because I come from a sceptical background. My father was quite anti-clerical. He was religious in his instincts – he prayed and read the gospels – but I never saw him in a church until the day he was in a coffin. I think it originated with his participation in the War of Independence, when he and others were allegedly excommunicated. Also, he knew and didn't like the old clericalism, yet he had personal friends among priests and nuns. My mother was from Waterford city and her mother was a church organist for fifty years, so there was a lot of conventional practice on that side. At this stage of my life – and perhaps all of my life – I find myself leaning in that direction and am basically comfortable with my position.

I find it very difficult to think of a personal God. I envy those who have a 'personal relationship' with God. That is beyond me, so far. I prefer to think of having a profound intuition rather than faith. What we call 'faith' is not simply a matter of an 'on' or 'off' switch; I think most people experience it as more akin to a dimmer switch that can wax or wane according to circumstance and lived experience – sometimes brighter, sometimes dimmer.

The religious instinct is a universal human thing through all ages and cultures, however it may be professed. Even when people profess quite aggressive atheism, to me that is a kind of religion. They would deny that of course, but it's still a response to the existential question. I wrote about this in a poem called 'Believers', a dialogue with a self-professed unbeliever:

Your unbelief seems stronger than my faith,
as though securely founded on a rock
from which you may believe with certainty
in some no-God, ineffably not there,
nor needing to exist or to explain –

and this becomes your clear theology
though no more free of its own mystery
than my uncertain intuition's reach
through sign and ritual towards some One
you've made the core of all your unbelief.

We both acknowledge earth and sea and stars
and know both good and evil in the world,
the gravity and grace of love and grief –
all that is seen and all we cannot see,
over and under, beyond and between.[1]

I don't profess absolute certainties. I prefer being creatively uncertain, what Keats called 'negative capability' – the idea that you are open to everything. Even a glance at creation makes it impossible for me not to believe that there is some kind of purpose and meaning to it all and that there is a creative being called God. I find that expressed in the institutional religion of the Catholic tradition and that is like an old coat that I wear with comfort. That said, I am critical of the institution in many ways. I like liturgy and ritual and am quite conservative regarding the part that liturgy played in the past; for example, plainchant, polyphony, great art. I can get a wonderful spiritual experience from listening to Mozart, Bach, Handel or Palestrina, which will lift me. One of the sad results of Vatican II – which had many admirable outcomes – was a cultural debasement of sacred music, which still lingers. Being 'happy clappy' embarrasses me

---

1. Previously unpublished.

and does nothing for me. Sacred music is a great sustenance to me and I could never lose that. Equally, there is a deep human need for ritual. It helps us manage the unmanageable in our lives.

In my teenage years I struggled with the hormones, as all teenagers do. I found tensions in Confession. There was such extraordinary emphasis on 'the flesh', which seems absurd now. There was this odd thing about Irish Catholicism – the idea that the body was evil and that woman was the source of evil. It looks pretty heretical now, but it might have been a post-Famine thing where catastrophe was a combination of blight, over-population and a certain lackadaisical pre-Famine attitude to breeding. Maybe as a result, the clergy were one of the agencies trying to impose social control? The pendulum has now swung the other way towards a non-judgemental morality. In between, we had the papal encyclical on birth control, *Humanae Vitae*, which was, to my mind, a total disaster.

The strengthening of my belief in adulthood probably has something to do with my capacity as a writer and a creature of the imagination and of memory. I believe that religious sensibility is connected to the human imagination and if you lose that connection it is almost a kind of lobotomy of the imagination. Anyone involved or interested in the arts is thereby involved in the transcendent, in my view. And the notion that science and religion are diametrically opposed is totally erroneous. I am interested in astronomy and am continually astounded and amazed by the almost everyday discovery of new mysteries in the universe. Fifty years ago we thought there was only one galaxy – the Milky Way – but now we know there are billions of them. We hear of dark matter and an expanding universe. Rather than that knowledge dismissing religion and saying 'This is science', it does quite the opposite for me. I am just in awe at the wonder and extraordinary beauty and depth of creation on both the macro and the micro scales.

When I was growing up, the expectation was that you believed everything literally, but one of the great cultural gifts that religion gave to me was an ease with symbolism and symbolic language. When I started to view what I was participating in as metaphor, it made things much easier for me. Metaphor isn't some kind of lie, but rather a gateway to perception.

As a writer I find that words can lift me just as much as the music of Bach and Mozart. I have a rather eccentric habit when I go to Mass – I answer some of the prayers aloud in the languages of my experience, for example in Latin (*Sursum corda, Habemus ad Dominum, Dignum et justum est*, the *Agnus Dei*) or in Irish (*Ár nAthair*) just to savour the words. I find some of the modern translations for parts of the Mass painful to hear. In an effort to be contemporary, they have impoverished the Mass for me. I prefer the old language. It carries a resonance, when the actual form in which something is expressed is inseparable from the content. Yeats said it much better in 'Among School Children':

O body swayed to music, O brightening glance,
How can we know the dancer from the dance?[2]

Words and their shape are very significant for me and I can be suddenly startled by something I may have been hearing all my life. I remember hearing the gospel at Mass one day, telling how Christ offered his wounds to Thomas as evidence of his human reality. Out of that came a poem, 'The Club', which is about how we all acquire wounds and graduate into 'the club' as we live:

You don't realise until you're forty or so
that by then everyone of your age or more
is walking around with some old wound that's buried
back of the eyes or somewhere under the coat.

---

2. W. B. Yeats, 'Among School Children', *The Tower* (1928).

Even then you forget that some of those you pass
with a nod every day on the road took their hits
quite early on, though you may not remember ever
seeing them stumble or fall or hearing them moan,

since that was before the water cleared to show
that wounding seems part of some general plan, with rules
that are not just bloody unfair, they're bloody unknown.
Strange how it took so long for the light to dawn

that sooner or later your own due turn would come
to take one in the shoulder or the gut,
entitling you to limp into the club,
a member in good standing, now fully paid-up.[3]

I try to pray formally, with varying success, but then I am also praying if I am listening to Palestrina. Prayer is a mysterious and deep concept. Who am I talking to? Am I talking? Simone Weil, a Jewish woman who was one of the great Christian thinkers, said prayer was paying absolute attention. Sometimes if I cannot sleep, one of my mantras is the *Salve Regina* – I maybe even imagine I'm chanting it. It is one of the great prayers which I love dearly. Even in the English translation there are lovely lines like 'Hail our life, our sweetness and our hope.' I grew up singing *Salve Regina* and those Benediction hymns – they touched our lives. That may be nostalgic, but so what? I like the Mass and go to weekday Mass regularly. It is a communal gathering which is a wonderful way of keeping a finger on the pulse of the little community I am living in. Of course it is about the mystery of the Eucharist which, being human, I cannot explain, but that doesn't make it any less rich for me. It is something that has evolved through human experience over a long, long time.

---

3. Michael Coady, 'The Club', *All Souls* (Oldcastle: The Gallery Press, 1997).

While I may be nostalgic for some hymns, there is a whole lot of the Catholicism of the past that I wouldn't want back – the clericalism which has done the Church great harm, the whole dark thing about the body and the danger that is in women. Yet I see that what is left of a tottering institution is being upheld by women. The clergy are dying on their feet. One of the things that Vatican II didn't change was the governance of the Church, which is frozen now. Maybe Pope Francis will make a difference but I cannot wait to see women ordained. It angers me greatly to see ordination denied to women. It is indefensible and unsustainable.

I have no idea of what lies beyond this life. I cannot believe there is nothing. I think it must be much more difficult to believe that 'this is it', as some rationalists profess. Philip Larkin wrote a fine poem called 'Church Going', in which he wonders what it will be like when all the churches fall out of use. In all his poetry, Larkin was sceptical and scathing, but at the end of this poem, he says of the church he is standing in:

> A serious house on serious earth it is,
> In whose blent air all our compulsions meet,
> Are recognised, and robed as destinies.
> And that much can never be obsolete,
> Since someone will forever be surprising
> A hunger in himself to be more serious,
> And gravitating with it to this ground,
> Which, he once heard, was proper to grow wise in,
> If only that so many dead lie round.[4]

Myself, I like to go into my local church when it is empty. There is a pregnant silence, a sense of generations past with all the significant landmarks and milestones of lives lived.

---

4. Philip Larkin, 'Church Going', *Collected Poems*, Anthony Thwaite, ed. (London, Faber and Faber, 2003).

As for the afterlife, I hope we will all know one another. Dying is the great adventure into the unknown and, while we don't know what the next life will bring, we at least have intuition. The Dalai Lama has said that all the great religions of the world are trying to climb the same mountain, but from different directions. There is hardly a culture in the world that doesn't have a religion – not all of them benign, but then Christianity itself was not too benign at times. The great fallacy of every age is that it thinks it is the pinnacle of enlightenment and looks on the past condescendingly. This is highly questionable, in my view. Purgatory is in some ways a more interesting concept than hell. We have to go through phases of enlightenment. Then there is the whole mystery of retribution. Just as there is good in the world, so also there is evil. So who will pay the price at the end of the road? Frankly, we have no idea, although Christian faith includes the idea of the mercy of God. To our human way of looking at injustice, it might seem a bit unfair that someone could get away with evil-doing and be forgiven, but one of the most profound things I know are Christ's words of forgiveness on the cross, which are simply staggering. Even if you have difficulty in understanding Christ as God, it is still staggering, as indeed is the whole Christ story.

It is the fact of death that makes religion relevant – the existential wondering about what is out there, why are we here, where are we going. I love Handel's *Messiah*, not just for its music but for the beautiful text and the theology therein:

> Behold, I tell you a mystery:
> We shall not all sleep;
> but we shall all be changed,
> in a moment, in the twinkling of an eye,
> at the last trumpet!

The mystery is as great as it ever was. The Dalai Lama also said that a man in search of enlightenment should know his own tradition first and then search out others. I consider that sound advice. The recent downgrading of speculative theology is a big sadness for me. Theology is all about ideas and I find ideas exciting. The exclusion of people like Hans Küng and the silencing of priests in this country are upsetting.

I am very comfortable with the sense of values that my faith encompasses. Paul sums it up: 'And now faith, hope, and love abide ... and the greatest of these is love.' That is the core of the Christian ideal. The core values are pointing towards some ultimate unification when all will be one. The Creed says it all, really: 'I believe in all things visible and invisible.' Great literature has always influenced me. *The Great Gatsby* has touched me at different stages of my life. I took the last sentence – 'So we beat on, boats against the current, borne back ceaselessly into the past' – as the epigraph for my most recent book, *Going By Water*. It's a metaphor for the journey of life, I suppose.

OLIVE DONOHOE

Olive Donohoe was born and raised in the Catholic faith in Dublin. She was educated by nuns and later at Trinity College Dublin, where through her experience as a bell ringer she was attracted to the Protestant tradition. Having worked as an inspector of taxes, she found her true vocation in ministry and eventually became a Church of Ireland rector. She has ministered in counties Cork and Laois and is currently rector in Athy, Co. Kildare.

All my life I have had a sense of reaching out to the sacred. Apparently when I was seven I announced to my parents – both devout Roman Catholics – that I was going to be a Methodist missionary! Where I picked that thought up I don't know, but I was quite happy with it at the time. On reflection, it could well have been a child's misunderstanding of the Medical Missionaries [of Mary].

I grew up in Dublin in a traditional Catholic home, one of five children. My parents practised their faith and brought all of us to Sunday Mass in the Capuchin church in Church Street. I can even remember some of their sermons to this day, which is a tribute to their priests. I went to a convent school, so I was very aware of spiritual things. For a year in secondary school we had a very go-ahead post-Vatican II nun for religious knowledge. We read the Bible every day in sixth class. I didn't understand a lot of it but some of the stories were great.

My father was a deeply spiritual man. He joined the Third Order of St Francis and when he retired he went to Mass daily – one day for each of us because we had gradually stopped going, the younger ones following the example of the older ones. There was one rule: you had to justify to him why you didn't go! In his heart he was a farmer, but he worked for Aer Lingus. He owned thirteen acres in Cavan and every weekend and every holiday we would squeeze into the old Morris van with cats, dogs and guinea pigs and off we went to our country retreat. I grew to love nature and the countryside. My father used to say that a cow was just like a poem!

At secondary school there was still a strong spiritual involvement. We had lovely retreats with long-haired Redemptorists playing guitar, and religion addressed for us the real issues of life. That was when I first came across Leonard Cohen. There was a song of his in the new-style religious knowledge textbook and I became a great fan, and I am still a fan. At the age of seventeen I went to Trinity College Dublin. I hadn't a clue what to do and chose science. By that time my faith was in abeyance but I realised a long-standing ambition by joining the Trinity Guild of Bellringers, who rang in St Patrick's Cathedral. I wasn't a great bellringer but it was my first real encounter with another denomination, of which I knew very little. The ambience of the cathedral and the beautiful evensong service really appealed to me. I was reaching out to the sacred again.

We were in and out of many churches – Christchurch, Bray, Blessington – where I felt at ease more and more. This was for me. I felt all the reforming had been done and I would be happier there, so I just switched. It wasn't the case at all that I had been an angry young Catholic. It wasn't that big a jump, in my view – more a change of tradition than one of religion. I didn't engage in the practice of the Protestant faith until I later joined a parish – St Anne's in Dawson Street, where Canon Adrian Empey was the vicar. I became part of the congregation and really enjoyed it.

On graduation from Trinity College, I trained as an accountant, but this was the 1980s, a period of recession, and jobs were hard to find. My dream was to have a book- and coffee shop in West Cork, keep a few cows and do accounts and taxation, but instead I joined the Civil Service and worked as an inspector of taxes for five years. Around that time, the Church of Ireland decided to ordain women. I had been favourably influenced by the rectors I had met and decided to apply. I felt 'the call' as a kind of knowing. Now I knew what I wanted to do. I prepared for two years with others in a 'fellowship of vocation'. This was to test your vocation. There followed a selection conference – a week-long residential interview by bishops and academics. I was in shock when I got the letter telling me I had been selected.

I studied for three years in theological college and did another year in All Hallows, pursuing a Master's degree in pastoral leadership. I loved being a student again. It was such an interesting course, offering a whole new awareness of God and his love. I went to Istanbul and Northern Ireland on placement. It was just a wonderful time and I never had any doubts about the path I had chosen. I was where I wanted to be.

When I was doing the course in All Hallows, we had to write an essay on 'The God I Believe In'. I asked a fellow student about this and she said, 'Don't be ridiculous. We can't be writing that kind of thing. We're Anglicans!' More recently I was discussing the notion of God with my bishop and he said, 'I believe that we are gathered into the heart of God, whatever that is.' That appeals to me greatly. I love the 'gathering in' aspect of it. We have to leave behind the childhood images we had of God. The problem is that we make God in our image rather than accept that he makes us in God's image. So much of what we believe is bound up in mystery and I accept that. That is why I love science. We don't know everything. I love the idea of mystery. It means we still have things to find out.

I can see people in the early centuries of the Church trying to understand this new revelation of God and trying to reconcile it to what they already know. This new doctrine is built up to give them something to hang on to, but it's not the whole picture. I love the icon of the Trinity in the *Hospitality of Abraham* – a famous icon by Andrei Rublev which depicts Abraham entertaining the angels without knowing it. The three persons of the Trinity are seated in a triangular pattern. It's very stylised and very beautiful.

Icons are coded to help people pray and reflect. I have become fascinated with icons. I do an icon retreat very year. I love the way icons work – they lead you further into the subject, like windows within windows.

I remember reading a book during my training, *Who You Are Is How You Pray*. It suggested that your particular temperament would draw you to a particular kind of prayer. Some are drawn to contemplative prayer, others are drawn to formal prayer. I am a conversationalist. I chat away to God all day about whatever I am doing or whatever is on my mind. I would pray more formally at night. I have a nun friend who is a prison chaplain. She spoke to us in Mountmellick. 'In prayer,' she said, 'you gather all your worries and intentions and at night bring them to the foot of the cross. Take them off and leave them there, at the foot of the cross with Jesus. Don't pick them up and put them back on again! Leave them with Jesus.' To me that was the most comforting thing. One of the big reasons for unbelief and loss of faith is unanswered prayer. Billy Graham's wife had the solution to that: 'It's just as well God doesn't answer prayer all the time,' she said. 'If he did, I would be married to the wrong man three times!' Personally, I try to pray about the situation rather than present a list of favours required.

My life is my faith now. I derive great satisfaction from being a rector. I love the variety of the work; you never know what is going to happen in any one day. You are there in the most important moments in people's lives – be it the joy of a new baby, a wedding, when people are dying, a funeral – and it is a very deep sharing. It's not that you may be doing very much, but ministry for me is presence, just to sit and be with people and share high and low points in their lives. I know this from my own experience. I had been very ill after a bypass operation and I loved when people visited me and sat with me, sometimes reading to me. It was so comforting. And of course the most successful visits are the short ones. The present Archbishop of

Armagh, Richard Clarke, visited my mother in hospital. She was dying but we didn't know it at the time. He had a lovely gentle approach and said, 'Eva, would you like me to say a prayer with you?' It's an approach I have since adopted myself – it makes things easier for both parties. I had major tragedy in my own life five years ago when my beloved George died. He took his own life. It broke my heart, both literally and metaphorically. The cardiac bypass fixed the literal part and the metaphysical part is slowly mending, but I never felt anger with God. I accept the human condition as it is. It must include the good and the bad, the joys and the tragedies, difficult as the latter are. Our culture today associates being human with being happy but I take the broader view.

I have no fear of death. George's death helped me in that regard. I don't feel I will be alone. I will be gathered up into the heart of God. That is enough for me. As humans we cannot know everything and that includes the afterlife. I like the image of the many rooms in the Father's house. Our limited minds need images like that. I often think about seeing loved ones again. Of course I would love to see them but it doesn't bother me because I know it will be all right. Whatever it is will be enough. As regards hell, I doubt if it will be fire and brimstone but again I don't know what awaits evildoers. I still wrestle with the problem of evil and with the notion of bad things happening to good people. There is hell on earth for many people. We speak from a very comfortable position in the West.

The time I spent in Turkey with the Christian Churches Refugee Project still haunts me. It was my first real experience of poverty and desperation. I saw children of eight to ten years of age who walked from Kuwait at night for a month to escape the Gulf War. That changed my life and I still wrestle with the suffering that is in the world. There is a famous Christian Aid cartoon consisting of three frames. In frame one a man says, 'I wonder why does God let all those awful things happen in the world'. In frame two, his friend says, 'So do I. Why don't you ask God?' In frame three the first man says, 'I'm afraid God might ask me the same question ...' That speaks to me. When you look at an ill-divided world, it is so not because of God but because people refuse to share.

The harder part of helping in the world is staying at home and trying to change people's outlook and attitudes. As a rector, I try to provide spiritual homework towards finding a response to a world in need. This week my parishioners' homework is to find some way to rock the boat. I'm looking forward to their answers to that! We also have outreach projects with the TRUST homeless charity and the Mendicity Institute in Dublin. The people make a commitment to provide necessities to these charities and, as the bishop says, the 'patient continuance' of this is the important thing.

I often thought of writing a book on people I consider to be saints. Alice Leahy of TRUST would be one; Walton Empey, former Archbishop of Dublin, who is a deeply pastoral person; Gordon Linney for his integrity and courage; the Reverend Bill Johnson and his wife, who spent thirty-three years in South Africa and left a huge legacy, not just in the people they loved and minded but in practical projects like a dam, a school which has forty computers donated from an Irish school and a children's village for AIDS orphans. That is real Christianity. These are real saints to me. I tell the children in my sermon to look at the figures in the stained-glass windows. They are saints, I say, because you can see through them! It's true because transparency is a big part of people who love in that way. I am also drawn to contemplative people. It wouldn't suit me temperamentally but the idea that around the world there are people praying for us is wonderfully supportive.

If I could have accompanied Jesus in his time, I would love to have been there in the desert when he and his disciples just talked of an evening. And to have been at the Last Supper –

without knowing it was the Last Supper. I love the Christian aspect of hospitality when everyone is invited to a feast. I have tried to develop that in the parish with tea and biscuits after the service. The people have learned the importance of breaking bread together. The liberation theologian Leonardo Boff spoke of the 'sacrament of the cup of tea'. For me, the ministry of tea and friendship is so important because it can open up so much more and is so worthy in itself.

In terms of faith I suppose I have come a long way from the indifference of youth. As I get older I get worried because there doesn't seem to be enough time to do all the things I want to do. I don't have the gift of contentment but neither do I have great discontent. I am wiser, I hope, and I sit more easily with myself than when I was young. The words of Micah set the standard for all of us: 'What does the Lord require of you but to do justice, and to love kindness, and to walk humbly with your God?' Reaching and holding that standard is the problem, of course. Those desperate children in Turkey still haunt me, all these years later.

MARK PATRICK HEDERMAN

Mark Patrick Hederman is a native of County Limerick. He is former headmaster of the Benedictine school at Glenstal Abbey, and is now the Abbot of Glenstal. He holds a doctorate in the philosophy of education and is a regular commentator and speaker on education matters. A former co-editor of The Crane Bag Journal of Irish Studies, *he is a prolific author whose works include* I Must Be Talking to Myself: Dialogue in the Roman Catholic Church Since Vatican II *(2004),* Symbolism *(2008),* Dancing with Dinosaurs: A Spirituality for the 21st Century *(2011) and* The Boy in the Bubble: Education as Personal Relationship *(2013).*

I have no recollection of not knowing God. I grew up on a farm and as a family we were very much on our own until I went to school at the age of nine. I suppose nature was the primary source of my knowledge. I remember walking down the avenue, knowing that God was addressing me and I was addressing him. He was a presence, not a man with a beard, and in no way frightening or unusual, somewhat like seeing a deer in a field and the moment it sees you it's gone.

I didn't grow up in a faith-filled home. My father didn't seem to believe in much, religiously speaking, and was horrified at my joining a monastery ('Why wouldn't you do something useful and become an actor?'). My mother was very much into mysticism but we never discussed it. She was keen that her children would do what they wanted to do. My sister and I were prepared privately for First Communion by Sr Julian. I had big arguments with her about God. She said to me, 'I hope when you reach my age you will be able to say "I've never committed a mortal sin", like I am saying to you now.' I replied, 'Are you not committing the sin of pride this minute?' The God Sr Julian was trying to tell me about had nothing to do with the 'presence' that was surrounding me. The Catholic Church has inflicted this God on people – an abusive monster that sent his only son into the world in order to torture him sufficiently to pay for the amount of disobedience and disrespect that we as creatures had inflicted on God the Father. I find that most people have an image of God as an all-powerful judge, which is a most horrific projection of our own worst fears of ourselves that we project onto the Trinity.

My understanding of the Trinity is so well conveyed by William Blake's beautiful picture where the Father received the Son after his crucifixion, with the Spirit hovering above. We crucified the God of Love because we were so terrified of love coming into the world. Those three persons form an amazing community, who were initially everything – the whole reality that is. In order to allow us to exist, they had to restrict themselves, almost provide a space within which something other than God could manifest itself. That is the reality of creation, which was probably as much a surprise to them as it was to us, and which gives us the extraordinary co-existence of the created and the uncreated worlds. God is simply love. We have been told that for over two thousand years. When Jesus Christ, who is God Incarnate, met anyone, the first thing he said was 'Don't be afraid'. God is love – a much-abused word, but if you have ever loved anybody you know what it means. Here in Glenstal we say to the parents of our students, 'No matter how much you love that child, it could not be anything like the way God loves you. That is your best way of understanding what God the Father is, how much he is longing for you.' God is love.

I joined the monastery in Glenstal, where I had been a boarder, simply to find a place where I could be with God. Glenstal seemed as good a place as any and still remains that. It is, I feel, where God wants me to be, an ideal location in terms of nature and liturgy. When I get up in the morning there is an already prepared framework for praise of God worked out for me. It is like an iron lung, an artificial way of making it possible for a human being to be in connection with God all day long. For others it may seem like a straitjacket to start your day singing psalms for an hour, but for us it provides the perfect structure for connecting with God, and once you get used to it, this is the language you want to learn. Singing is one of the most basic gifts that any culture possesses. In the slave trade, when people were separated to prevent them talking when working, they learned to sing instead, whether as road gangs or mothers nursing children. We are a singing people and singing praise is a much more basic activity than talking or thinking. In Glenstal, we sing Gregorian chant, which is hundreds of years old and has an effect on the bloodstream. I once travelled in a New York taxi where the driver played a CD of Gregorian chant, explaining: 'My shrink told me to use it for road rage!'

Glenstal has nourished me as a person. My faith has not changed one iota from when I was seven, but the monastery has nurtured my own faith and being to such an extent that I am now aware of what I didn't know before in an intellectual way. I can now put words on what was a natural and instinctive thing from my childhood.

One of my great faith mentors was the Jewish philosopher Emmanuel Levinas. I met him in Paris when I studied theology there. For Levinas, the primary focus of philosophy was ethical responsibility for the Other. Philosophy, he would say, is the wisdom of love rather than the love of wisdom. I am convinced that God provides us with a book or a person that we need at a particular moment to understand him, so books often just fall into my hands at the right time. When I was studying here in the novitiate, I came across the complete works of Karl Jung. They were by no means recommended reading at the time but they were very important to me. Iris Murdoch's work was hugely influential throughout my spiritual growth and I was very privileged to meet her. Dostoyevsky and Rilke have probably influenced me more than any particular human being that I have happened to be alive with. At this time of my life the novels of Colum McCann are speaking to me.

You may be thinking it's a long way from Jung to McCann but there are people who have the gift of recording what a culture is going through and if you don't make yourself aware of what they are saying, you are leaving yourself behind. Every Irish person needs to read James Joyce because he was a great prophet who taught us all just how shallow our Catholicism was. Likewise, John McGahern, who for me is our Kafka and Proust rolled into one. He explained to us the Ireland of the 1950s in relation to our parents, as they were the archetypes of the time. Colum McCann is an Irishman who went to America and understands the links between the two countries, portraying them in a most imaginative and creative way. His greatest novel for me is *This Side of Brightness*. He is so engaged with what is going on underground and this is nourishment for my soul. Jung was saying way back that we need to go underground into our unconscious – something we Irish never did and never wanted to do until now. It's only through our novelists and poets that we do so, so it's not really a long way from Jung to McCann!

People regard darkness as dangerous or different, but it represents half of our life. Problems arise when we try to pretend it's all bright. One of the symbols of the newly independent Ireland was *An Claidheamh Soluis*, the Sword of Light, when Ireland was meant to be the brightest place on the planet. That's not enough – there are two sides to every story. Whereas other cultures like Russia over-emphasised the dark and the underside of the human condition, the whole project of de Valera and John Charles McQuaid's Ireland was to create a First Holy Communion dress for all of us, which would make us the envy of the planet. It was a disaster. By concentrating on the white and pure, everything went underground. We now see the chaos that was caused by not examining the other side of ourselves and what that meant for families and institutions. We had the same time span as Communist Russia (starting 1916–17). The Russians produced gulags and all the horrors of concentration camps. We produced a similar kind of horror that has recently emerged. All those inner life forces that we refused to deal with or to admit their presence developed a monstrous life of their own. All I am saying is that we must examine the darkness, the unconscious, that half of our lives spent in the sleep and dream world (which is exactly what Joyce was doing in *Finnegans Wake*) in order to create the balance necessary to provide a lifestyle that will be total.

I loved the way the Dalai Lama replied when asked how often a day he meditated: 'I am constitutionally incapable of meditation.' Brilliant! There are all sorts of meditation techniques which are really a kind of mental hygiene, an attempt to quieten the frenetic mind. Contemplation is very different. It is connecting everything to God. It's very like the instruction to the acrobat on the tightrope – whatever you do, don't look at your feet! Peripheral vision is what is required. Keep your eyes wide open to see what is coming and how it connects. Thomas Merton said connection is contemplation. The metaphysical poets, like John Donne, connected most unusual things that people don't associate with one another. That's what the monks are there for – to say how God connects with what is going on in our world today. It's a bit like holding the newspaper in one hand and the Bible in the other. We supply the ventilation, the connection with God, keeping the borehole open so that people will know what their lives mean at this time in terms of what God is trying to achieve.

I see faith as being flexible rather than solid. Most people would see faith as a list of things you believe in, as in the Apostles' Creed, but for me there are just three things: faith, hope and love. And the greatest of these is love. Faith is love and connection. I feel that connection with God all the time. It hasn't grown or increased because it is the same as it always was, but this monastery feeds it and allows it to be more alive. Your mind cannot be connected with God all the time, but here during the day there are sufficient reminders which allow you to be still on the watch. The institution is only there to provide a runway as it were, for the real connection with God, which is mostly wordless. Silence is really the language that God speaks, and often it can be a difficult medium for us to deal with. You are not meant to fill silence with words but with a loving attention. 'Speaking' to God is extending your attentive presence to a darkness which is a form of the presence of God. You become aware of it and try to maintain that communication. For me that may last at most a quarter of an hour in the morning and in the evening. Sometimes I attempt to force God's hand, pleading and arm-twisting him, and it works if it's meant to be. Every day I spend time in front of our healing icon with others, and that can be a huge energy of prayer. The number of people who have found help and healing from it is quite impressive.

Like most people, I fear suffering, incapacitation and dependence on others, but I don't fear death at all. I feel a huge connection with those who have died and gone to God, especially at the Eucharist when we are linked with the Communion of Saints. Death is just another part of the adventure. For me, the great symbol of life is the butterfly. We have three stages in our life: in the womb, in the world and then the world to come. I find this quite natural and see it reflected in nature. And I see the connection with God in people outside the monastery, people who maybe don't have the advantages of education or wealth but are connected with God in a way that is impressive to me.

And after death, the ultimate prize! We are created beings and so have time and space limits that God does not have. We are told by Jesus and the Holy Spirit that we are being given the opportunity of becoming eternal through this connection with

God, who is love. The divine energy will keep us going forever. We don't know exactly what this means but I don't care how it will happen. That is a mystery that God will make happen. I don't ask myself what age I will be for eternity. I just know that wherever God is, he will want me to be there too. I have no doubt that my loved ones can't wait for me to join them in eternity. I don't find they are absent from me, even now. The great message of the Ascension was Christ's words to Mary Magdalen: *Noli me tangere*, do not touch me. Let me go in my physical human frame and let me reach another place prepared since the beginning of time where I will bring you to me.

There is no forcing us to love. There is an option to be unloved, to be our own sweating selves, as Hopkins says. And that is hell. There are people on this planet at this moment who are in hell because they refuse to love anybody. All that fire and burning stuff is nonsense. The great challenge is that we can love or not love. Hell is a state of no love. Heaven is where we are open to others.

I am grateful now for the faith I have and the God I believe in. I don't think I was always grateful for everything I received, which was enormous. Gratitude is something you learn and it is the way of being which we are most at home in. That's what the Book of Psalms is all about – praise and gratitude. It's not really possible to praise and thank, unless you believe in God. When you do, that is the most appropriate and most satisfying stance you can take. I certainly am happy to take that stance and to create a life in a monastery where praise and thanks constitute the meaning and structure of our lives.

FRANK KELLY

Frank Kelly was born in Dublin and educated at Blackrock College and University College Dublin. He qualified as a barrister but chose acting as a profession. Now a veteran of stage, screen, radio and television, he is probably best known as Father Jack in the hugely successful television series Father Ted. *As a measure of his versatility, he has also topped the record charts with his version of 'The Twelve Days of Christmas'.*

The God I believe in is the God I was taught about in childhood, but of course he has developed into a huge presence and power in my life. I didn't think like that as a child, obviously. I liked the story of Bethlehem when we celebrated the birth of Christ and we got nice toys to play with. Like most children, I thought of my religion as a pretty story. We were encouraged to do so in mid-twentieth-century Ireland.

I didn't grow up in an overly-religious house. It was more a thinking house. The standard of debate was very high at the dinner table as we came into our teens. You would have to choose your words carefully or my father would challenge you. He was a very intelligent man – a highly-ranked civil servant who also ran *Dublin Opinion* magazine for many years. He had a very direct and devotional attitude to religion. For some reason, he was very keen on our being in time for Mass, but he wasn't a religious fanatic otherwise. The Knights of Columbanus made repeated attempts to enlist him, but he would not have anything to do with them. He thought the Church was quite adequate for a Christian who was a Catholic, without having to be members of pressure groups or organisations within that Church. My mother was deeply religious, but she had a very sacred sense of humour. Once when she went to Blackrock church it was under repair. She was confronted by a big sign 'DO NOT ENTER! EXTREME DANGER!'

A huge block of granite was suspended over the entrance by a chain. Despite pleas from workmen, she walked right in. 'I like to live dangerously!' she said. She was a wonderful woman.

I spent a number of years as an altar boy. Not through any piousness on my part – I was introduced to it by someone else. I served in the Carmelite convent in Blackrock. It was an excellent introduction to religious services because the nuns were very economical in what they did. The prayers were very clear and the Mass was simple and to the point. The focus was on the Consecration and Communion. The whole experience had a great and lasting effect on me.

For all that, I was a bit of a 'wide boy' at school. I might be serving Mass, but I would dodge school retreats, smoke butts and sneak out into the woods of Blackrock College. I was too cool for retreats – I had too much of an eye for the girls! At one of the few retreats I did attend, we had a Redemptorist priest lecturing us on hell through Brueghelian art. It was all about people running around with tridents stuck in their bare bottoms, snakes devouring them, with others being thrown off high ledges into devouring flames – all to show the utter agony of hell. He was in full flight but then stopped suddenly and said, 'One thing ... never be put off your faith by a silly priest!' It was the most iconoclastic thing a schoolboy could say then, let alone a Redemptorist. It has stayed with me ever since and from that moment my faith became my property and not that of the pope.

That experience helped me to stay in the fold and not to fool myself too much as I grew into adulthood. When I became aware of the enormous realities of the Big Bang theory and other incredible scientific discoveries, I realised that one had to choose between atheism and this other stream of belief, which by the extreme logical standards of science would look rather silly. I recognise that there is something ridiculous in believing the New Testament when the Big Bang theory is available, but the thing about faith is that it grows as you feed it. It becomes another reality and my faith now is not centred at all on Rome. It is a gift which has to be nourished as you would water a flower in the garden. I find the Mass tremendously fulfilling. The moment of Consecration matters enormously to me. Of course it is mystery – a very powerful mystery which I cannot explain. By the standards of scientists, what I am professing is ridiculous. I have to live with that. I sympathise with those who cannot believe, but not in any patronising way. I can live with mystery. One has little choice. You cannot take out a slide rule and measure eternity.

Coming into middle age, I neglected my faith for many years. I was very busy, professionally, and could not cope, so I pushed my faith to one side. I was having so many erotic thoughts – my mind was full of Brueghelian sexuality! With the advent of *Playboy* and such magazines, we were bombarded with erotic images, particularly when I worked in London. I let the whole faith thing float for years. I just didn't worry myself too much about it, although I did go to Mass most of the time. I have always hated a Mass-less Sunday. Without the focus of the Eucharist, Sundays seem featureless to me. I feel that way today if I am away on holiday and it is difficult to get to Mass. Then one day in my own kitchen I had a sort of road to Damascus moment. There was nobody in the house. The children, who were very young, were playing in the garden. I took down my violin and played for an hour until the smallest one needed to be fed. In that previous hour I had a serious chat with myself about the direction of my faith life. Everything was discussed, including my Brueghelian sexuality. What did I really treasure and believe? Was I prepared to continue? I came down on the side of faith.

My religion is not a worship of Rome. It is a picture of the road to Galilee, to Jerusalem, to Emmaus – that exciting and unique story of the birth of Christ and his journeys of healing, loving and forgiving people, in which he denounces violence and rapaciousness. That is the God I worship, and I follow in my mind with intense interest his story and that of the beginnings of our Church each time I attend Mass. My faith is therefore very enriching for me. It gives me a reason for living. I don't go around beating my breast or preaching my religion. Indeed, I would like to be a better example of it. I would like to be kinder and more forgiving – a thing I have always been bad at. I can still feel an injury from childhood as fiercely as the day I received it. I would like to be more Jesus-like, I suppose. I would want nothing more than to sit and watch the crowds flock to him in Galilee, Capernaum, Jericho, and to see their reactions to him. I love the fact of his modesty. If he drew too much of a crowd, he suggested that they move elsewhere. Then he fed that crowd.

I encounter doubts, as I think we all do, but I don't allow them to linger. My doubts centre more on the Church as an institution than on articles of faith. I have a lot of problems with the Vatican's procedures. As far as I am concerned, they deny human rights. If you are silenced, you need not know either who your accuser is or the full depth of the accusation. I am a trained lawyer, and to me that goes against natural justice. What has occurred at that level within the clergy is utterly, utterly appalling. I cannot see why they are not excommunicated, whereas if I say something revolutionary regarding liturgical matters, I can be excommunicated. My good friend Brian D'Arcy has been reprimanded for saying a few simple things, for example regarding women priests.

Regarding articles of faith, I accept them with some qualification. In the New Testament, some phenomena may or may not be adequately described or may have lost some of the original story because of the inability of the narrator to write it clearly. These are only superficial things and do not worry me. A lot of the Old Testament is incredible stuff, but again it doesn't worry me – it has nothing to do with the existence of God. For all that, and my own occasional erratic wanderings, my faith hasn't waned. Rather has it strengthened over the last thirty years and it is now central to my life and my work. My professional life as an actor is to me a 'vocation' just as strong as a call to the priesthood. Whatever talent I have is God-given and I am thankful for that. It has given me a good life and enabled my wife Barbara and me to rear seven children. I never wanted to be a Hollywood star or to be a millionaire, just to do what I do well and to keep doing it for a living. I have worked in a wide range of theatre and television productions and the role of Father Jack, the alcoholic priest in *Father Ted*, was just one role that blossomed in the public imagination – and I enjoyed it immensely!

Prayer is very important to me. I pray regularly. I allocate about ten minutes to formal prayer every morning, on my knees, hands joined. I don't pray for lists of things, but for the ability to achieve worthwhile things. I pray particularly for the souls of the departed and name the ones dear to me. I pray for friends who are troubled. Much of my prayer now is more of a conversation with Christ, rather than formal prayer. I don't meditate as such but I use time at the wheel of the car or in the doctor's or dentist's waiting room. I do a lot of thinking. That to me is a kind of prayer. I like to reflect on Jesus travelling the roads during his mission on earth. I love the evidence of his humanity, when he asks the Father to be spared suffering but he is denied that. He needed help to see it through to the end, thus illustrating the weakness of humanity.

If I could have accompanied Jesus on his travels, to be present at any event would do. I think of the woman about to be stoned to death for adultery, and Jesus charges them, 'Let he who is without sin cast the first stone.' That would have been an interesting and powerful moment. We have to remember that initially his followers were seen as a revolutionary dissident sect within the Jewish community. Jesus was also a formidable man because in the framework of civil society he drove the money changers out of the temple with a whip. He was no wimp! I see him as a strong man, probably due to carpentry work when Joseph was engaged in building a Roman fort. So I see him as a strong, forceful character (not quite the image we see in Sacred Heart pictures) whose example we should all try to follow.

Death frightens me. I suspect it frightens everybody. With a bit of luck I will die in a state of grace. It's a kind of religious roulette: will I have received the Sacraments when the call comes? Salvation will be another dimension to living, which will be eternal. We have a very short race to run here on earth. I don't have time to think about hell. Running around fearing hell is very negative. Fear played far too big a part in Catholicism in the past. Far too much fear, far too little love. I believe in an afterlife but I find it very hard to visualise. It is very difficult to see it as material, i.e. that we should all appear with perfect bodies on the Last Day. I reckon I will experience the departed again, but in what form? It's not really important to me. If I get on with the business of trying to remain in a state of grace and trying to worship my God as best I can, that will do for now. My belief has grown with years of commitment to it. I have that feeling that I am right to be where I am now in terms of faith and that I am going in the right direction.

My main concerns are with the administration and structure of the Church. I read an article recently which said, 'Central to our creed is belief in Jesus Christ as God incarnate, but nowhere in our creed do we profess our belief in the Vatican State, of whose origins and history we know practically nothing.'[1] I heartily agree. Yes, there needs to be an institution, a civil service, to manage an organisation of that size, a grouping of people who subscribe to Christ along the lines asked of them by him. But it's not about civil power. It's not about the Curia denying people their rights. I have a feeling that Pope Francis will change the shape of the Curia radically, if indeed he allows it to continue to exist in its present form. I hope to live to see change like that happening – it would please me greatly.

---

1. John Mannion, 'Faithful Should Distinguish Between Catholic Faith and Vatican State', *Irish Times* (21 September 2012).

PHYLLIS KILCOYNE

Phyllis Kilcoyne was born in County Sligo. She joined the Mercy Order after leaving school. She enjoyed a career as a science teacher and school principal before moving into the area of family therapy. In 2001 she became part of the Leadership Team of the Western Province of the Mercy Order. She is a regular speaker at retreats and spiritual gatherings.

The more I come to a greater understanding of the universe, the more it speaks to me of the wonder of God. My sense of God now is of one whose presence is always with me, but he is also the God of the extraordinary, evolving, magnificent universe.

I grew up in a small village in the west of Ireland, the eldest of three and the only girl. My parents were strong, church-going, faith-filled people, who lived their lives according to the values of truth, honesty and generosity. We prayed as a family but not in a ritualistic way. The rosary wasn't said every night, for example. The fields, bogs and wells were my playground. I went to a small two-teacher school and I was the only girl in my class. I had a lot of time on my own, which shaped me to be reflective and to be curious. The teaching was very limited. It was not a happy time. School didn't challenge me at all.

The God of my childhood was derived from what I heard in church and from what I experienced learning the commandments. He was a God to be feared. The eye of God was watching over you and if you didn't follow his way you would be punished. God was in charge and you had the choice of punishment or reward. I moved on to a Sisters of Mercy school for my secondary education. They were caring and interested in their pupils. I found myself in a new way. The new subjects opened me up in a whole new way and I really enjoyed this very different experience. The practice of religion in secondary school was not rigid but I was very influenced by visiting African missionaries; priests and sisters who talked to us about the missionary life and how they had answered the call to give their lives in service to God.

I had my first inklings of a vocation as a junior at secondary school. I wanted to use my gifts to help others. The spiritual side of my life was of growing importance. I joined the Mercy order straight from school, much to the disappointment of my mother. She felt I was too inexperienced and that I was unduly influenced by the nuns. Her own experience of nuns at primary school was quite negative – she experienced them as harsh and uncaring. When I made my decision she cried for weeks. My father accepted my choice and tried to hold the balance with my mother. She visited me often in the convent and told me I would always be welcome home. It was a difficult time for both of us. At one level, I thought I was doing a good thing. But at another level my choice was hurting her. It caused me to look at religious life from many angles. I questioned its practices, some of which were nonsensical, for example that of my superior reading my mother's letters before I received them. Was this the life I really wanted? I was challenged but I stayed with my choice in the end. The challenge continued into my thirties until I made a thirty-day retreat with the Jesuits. I decided there that the religious life was my true calling and I would give it everything I had. I have never looked back.

I taught science and eventually became a school principal, a job I really loved. It afforded me the opportunity to listen to the more vulnerable children and see if I could reach out to them. There was one particular case of a boy who was sexually abused at home. He came to me and told me his story. Many years later I was a witness when the family took a high court case against the father. When the judge asked the young man what the teacher had done for him, he replied, 'She heard my story.' There was absolute silence in the courtroom. It confirmed in me the necessity and the importance of what I had done.

Once I had made my decision at the retreat to continue to serve God as a Mercy sister, I came to know him in a different way. The God of fear was gone. I was aware of a personal, loving God, of whom I had an interior experience. I became more reflective and tried to do as best I could in my teaching life as an expression of my engagement with him. This period of my life coincided with the Second Vatican Council, which opened up a whole new exploration of what religious life and practices were all about. Personally, it gave me a new energy. Rather than being separated from society and living a monastic kind of life, I felt more and more a part of that society. My image of God was now more that of being a Good Samaritan. I didn't feel as guilty when I didn't measure up to his expectations.

My experience as a school principal had shown me how so many children could get lost in the school system because they could not cope with other issues outside of the school. I left teaching and turned to family therapy, which opened up a whole new world for me. It was difficult and very challenging work, dealing with violence and abuse within families, but I had and have no fear of managing those situations. Unearthing the truth brings freedom, and if I can help in that process, it is very rewarding. I also became involved with the Western Province Leadership Team, which brought me into contact with Mercy sisters from seven West of Ireland dioceses. I was seeing both the best and the weaker sides of humanity.

And then came the horrific stories from the orphanages and the Magdalene Laundries. When the Ryan Report was published, I felt deeply embarrassed and ashamed, but deep down I heard the pain in these stories. I suppose it was related to my relationship with my mother and her own experience. Over the years there was a sadness between us, almost an unspoken barrier, even though we were very caring of each other. I remember watching the orphanage story on television with her when she was in her nineties and in a nursing home. It helped me hear her story in a new way. It was an insight for me and a release for her, and it brought tears to us both. In a mysterious way I felt God was offering me this truth to help bring about a reconciliation in my heart with my mother. This indeed happened and I was with her when she died in 2004.

I had never worked in an orphanage but I talked with sisters who did. One could not but acknowledge the pain that was caused. I am happy that we, as an order, did apologise to the victims of abuse, but it still cast a big cloud over all our lives. I found myself dealing with sisters who were very vulnerable around the story. All of that lowered our energy considerably, but I do believe that good will always triumph over evil and the truth will always set us free.

Our opportunities as Mercy sisters are endless now. If there is an idea that we have that we would like to set up some little project or do something for any group in society, there are few regulations around that, but sadly our energy and our numbers are diminishing. There is the contradiction. When we were younger we had the energy but we felt restricted in what we could do. Now the reverse is the case.

My image of God now is very much that of a presence, more as a friend. A God who is everywhere, who is kindly towards us and very much still a God of mystery, something beyond life, beyond anything that happens. I am always surprised by daily happenings – little gifts and little hardships too – that come my way unexpectedly. Looking at a new day in a new way is part of being open to the God of surprises, the God of life, the God of mystery. I have moved away from trying to explain mystery in a rational way, because God is beyond human understanding. I am comfortable just to take each day as it comes and be thankful to God for that. Being grateful is an important part of my life, being grateful for things we often take for granted – health, a fine day, hopefully peace in Northern Ireland today [12 July].

We hear of so much violence and sadness in the world, but my belief is that good will eventually triumph over evil. How can I reconcile a loving God with violence and tragedy in the world? I have no answer to that. Does anyone? My father used to say, 'You can only play the hand you are given.' What is important is how I respond to what comes my way, hopefully in a loving rather than a negative, aggressive way.

Prayer is important in my life, but within our community so many of us pray in different ways that we only have formal community prayer on certain occasions. In earlier days there was a rigid monastic system imposed but that is gone now. Yes we have Eucharist and I love reading the Psalms, but otherwise I let the rhythm of the day fit in with me. I love quiet time in the morning for meditation, or a walk by the sea in the evening. I question myself. How can I manage situations? How can I live better? A questioning mind is to me a prayerful mind. Where is the good thing, the God thing, in this situation? Trying to offer a kind word, a listening ear, a gentle approach – all of that is prayer too. Prayer nowadays is more a conversation, a presence with a listening ear to the God of my heart, who is the author of all life. Over the years the pain around the relationship with my mother wounded me and caused me to falter in my faith many times, but now I am at peace with whatever comes my way. It really is a matter of taking one day at a time and trusting that God will give me the graces I need for that day.

Equally, I don't have a real fear of death – apart from a fear of pain or illness. I simply trust that God will give me the grace I need when that day comes. In the meantime, I live as best I can. I believe in an afterlife. I don't know what shape or texture it will take but as scripture has promised, it will be more beautiful and spirit-filled than anything we have known heretofore. Those who have departed before me will enjoy whatever I enjoy in whatever shape, and love will continue beyond death. I believe totally in the Communion of Saints – it will be wonderful. I don't accept there is a hell in the way we learned it at school. There is undoubtedly evil in the world and we must protect ourselves from getting caught up in it. So many people do so unknowingly and their lives become living hells. I cannot perceive what 'hell' will be like, but I trust that the God-spirit will deal with evil and that ultimately good will triumph.

My parents were obviously my first faith-mentors. My father was a gentle faith-filled man who had great respect for life. In the order, some of my superiors were strict, but there was one in particular who trusted me even when I questioned or disagreed with our practice. She recognised that I was questioning out of my truth rather than trying to knock anything down. As I look across the history of the Church, many saints impress me. But really Christ is the mentor of all mentors. When I say I believe in God I am also saying I believe in Jesus Christ as the revelation of God. I never tire of reading the scriptures. The stories of Christ's life offer so much wisdom and invitation to do good. They are a real source of energy and support for me.

If I could have accompanied Jesus for one day in his life on earth, I would like to have met him at Jacob's well with the Samaritan woman (this is probably influenced by my childhood when we were sent to draw water from the wells). I would have loved to converse with him. He was offering the water of eternal life, but had no bucket with him (Jn 4:11). I would like to gaze into the well and see my reflection or life story, as the Samaritan woman did. I would have talked to Jesus about my own life, helping me to make sense of it, looking at all the different parts of it with as wide open a heart as I could manage, uncovering little pieces I might have packed away – all without fear.

The nearest I have come to that is having a spiritual director, who would know me as I am, as I see myself before God. When I meet her I discuss all aspects of my life, not just the spiritual side but my health and emotional life as well. We grew up in a time when we separated body and soul. I see it as one now, all connected. Conversations with my spiritual director help me to knot things together. In recent times, I am in a position where I can offer similar support and guidance to other people. Allied to that is the commonality of purpose and support within the community. And if that were not enough, there is the Holy Spirit often giving me a little nudge like a gentle breeze. And of course Mary, whom I see as the great mentor of Jesus on earth. I pray to her for guidance, often while I am travelling, using the prayers of my childhood. All of these supports lead me to the God of all, the Uncontainable One.

When I look into the well of my life, I am happy with the decisions I made. In the midst of all the ups and downs, twists and turns, I am happy that there was a constant search in me for God. And God gives all of what we need, in whatever measure we need. When I take time to question, it all makes sense to me. Things fit.

ALICE LEAHY

Alice Leahy was born in County Tipperary and trained in Dublin to be a nurse. Her work with the Simon Community brought her into contact with the homeless and their need for medical and healthcare. She co-founded TRUST, a non-judgemental befriending, social and health service for the homeless. She is a regular commentator, broadcaster and lecturer on the needs of the outsider in society. She is the editor of With Trust in Place *(2003), an anthology of 'writing from the outside' to celebrate thirty years of TRUST (www.trust-ireland.ie).*

I grew up on a small holding near Fethard in County Tipperary. We didn't own the land; it belonged to the Hughes family of the 'big house'. But there was no 'us and them' situation; we treated each other with respect. Olivia Hughes became a great friend of mine and a great influence on my life. Five generations of my father's family had worked that holding and my father worked the land as if he owned it. He instilled a great respect for nature in me. At this time of year [February] the lambs were being born and the miracle of new life was all about us. God was in the fields and there was so much to wonder at. I was blessed with that wonder and with parents who had tremendous faith – in particular my mother who is hale and hearty today, aged ninety-four, and whose faith has never wavered. That faith permeated the whole community and stood to them in good times and bad. If we haven't got a belief, there is something missing in our lives. I wonder if that is what is wrong with our country today. Do we lack the sense of wonder and the faith and hope that we can create a better world? It almost seems fashionable to ridicule the wonderful gift of wonder that we are here in this world and alive.

We grew up with the Ten Commandments, the catechism and the gospels. It was very much a learn-by-heart religion. There was no questioning of things as there is today. There was a certain reassurance in prayer and ritual that God was there. It gave us a security, knowing that we were being protected and guided. We prayed to our Angel Guardian for protection in the night. The rosary was a nightly ritual. We always said grace before and after meals. Maybe there isn't as much formal prayer today, but there is something about being grateful for what we have – food on the table, clothes on our backs – just stopping for a minute to say thanks to this unknown entity, this wonderful force that is out there for our good and support.

As we grew up we learned the answers to such major questions as Who is God? and Where is God? from our catechism, and we were secure in our thinking about God the Father, but it was far easier to connect with Jesus – he lived here, he taught by his example, he suffered, he died. The Holy Spirit seemed to be the poor relation in all of this, but the Spirit is with us to guide us. There is huge mystery in all of this, of course. To paraphrase Bob Dylan, 'We're all prisoners living in a world of mystery'. Maybe we are prisoners in the sense of always doubting, searching, struggling. Doubting is a natural part of belief. If you think at all, you will always be doubting. Doubts can make you stronger and propel you on your journey. The only way to elevate them is by making time to wonder; to stand still and reflect in a busy world. Today's world is not conducive to reflection. Everybody is in a rush but I always try to find the time and space to reflect. I have a simple prayer I say every morning: 'Dear God, this is the day you have made and I am glad to be part of it.' I go on to seek the guidance of the Spirit for what we do. I can't really define God, but I can make the connection with Jesus and the Spirit.

I began my working life as a nurse and then worked with the Simon Community. I came across very broken people who inspired me to think a lot about medical and health care for the homeless. Eventually, together with a small group of interested people, I set up TRUST, a charity which would ensure that a health service would be available for the broken and the homeless. In an ideal world there would be no need for a charity like TRUST, but nearly forty years on we are meeting more people in need than ever. Homelessness is a very complicated problem. It can arise for all sorts of reasons – addiction, isolation, broken relationships, a sexuality that is not accepted – and from all sorts of backgrounds. Housing is not necessarily the solution. In fact, it may create a bigger problem. There are no easy answers. In some cases there are no answers but our philosophy is based on two central principles: 1. The recognition of every individual's right to be treated as an autonomous and unique human being; and 2. The need to restore the dignity of individuals whom society has labelled deviant and undesirable.

We live in a society that sees only the big impressive gestures. The small things are seen as irrelevant, but they are the things we do in TRUST. We welcome the abused, the broken, the lost, whose bodies are often ravaged by disease and violence. They come in for a wash, a change of clothes or simply for acknowledgement. We can't change the world, but we can maybe make life a little easier for others. My feeling is if people feel no worse off for having met us, then our work is worthwhile. Mother Teresa once said, 'The biggest sickness of the West is not TB or leprosy, it's loneliness.' The people who come to us say that all they need is to be acknowledged – we give them a smile, say hello, recognise them as persons. Nowadays everything is measured in time, and charities like ours would be seen by some as 'wasting time with people'. But if you can't spend time with people, how can you know their needs and the possible solutions to those needs? It is far better, in my view, to be 'wasting time with people' than to be forever discussing budgets and projects. Of course, we need certain levels of bureaucracy but we are coming down with it in this country. Fitting templates and ticking boxes is the easy thing to do but looking at what is in the box is much more important.

One of the people who came in to us over the years was Tony Gill. He was a real character and a poet. He wrote these lines:

> Today I spoke to no one
> And no one spoke to me.
> Am I dead?

That says it all about homelessness.

Every day I ask myself where is God in all of this and how can he allow such suffering in the world? I struggle a lot with that. I envy people who have the belief that all will be well. While I know the Lord works in mysterious ways – and we have daily evidence of that in TRUST – we also see terrible suffering, frustration, pain and addiction. Many addicts become so because there is no space for them to ask questions, and so they go more into themselves and take drugs to dull that pain. Maybe one good thing to come out of the recession is that more groups are coming together to pose questions. How can we create a community or a society where everyone is important and special? If you believe in God, everyone is important. Sometimes the structures put in place to look at poverty, or indeed religion, isolate people. How do we reach them? Certainly not by saying you are a sinner and God will forgive you if you go the right way. That is no different from the pat answers of the catechism we grew up with.

I like to think that on this February morning Jesus is outside in the front room of the TRUST building with our people. The place is full. Lyric FM is playing in the background. A candle gives a soothing atmosphere. The only religious item on the premises is a St Brigid's Cross. Jesus is like the people who come here. He wouldn't be down dealing with the bankers or in the Dáil chamber; he is sitting out there with the broken and the lost, saying nothing, observing. He is challenging the powers that be. He is challenging all of us to say it as it is. He was crucified, remember. If you speak out, you can be crucified in all sorts of ways – isolated, chastised by bureaucracy, as we have been on a number of occasions. But you are guided by the Spirit and it is a price worth paying, because we get the most amazing support from some of the most unlikely people in all walks of life.

I have always questioned all aspects of life and I think it is very important to do so. Being certain of anything can be dangerous. I gave a talk recently and a woman in the audience said, 'I know where I am going.' I told her she was very lucky! A priest friend of mine once warned me off going to Africa because he knew I was always asking questions and I would find the situation there too difficult and overwhelming. When I was on the Human Rights Commission, I was constantly asking why is legal expertise so important? Why is the language around human rights so different? I know I am difficult for a lot of people; for myself, even. The easiest thing in the world is to blame. The hardest thing is to remain positive and try to do something and to understand that there are some things you can do nothing about.

I ask questions of God also. I remember in the early 1980s I was unsure about my work with TRUST and I used pray every morning, 'Dear God, give me a sign that I should continue. Am I mad? What am I doing?' My mother asked me to visit a neighbour in Cappagh Hospital. As I got off the bus I saw an old woman with a little girl, pulling a heavy case. I advised her to talk to the nun inside about somewhere she might stay. As we entered, a fellow jumped over the gate and grabbed my handbag. I shouted after him, 'I work with people like you.' If I hadn't been there he would have attacked the old woman and the shock might have killed her. A journalist friend of mine wrote a piece in the paper about the incident. That afternoon the bag was handed into Cappagh Hospital with a note: 'Sorry for the trouble'. The next day I was on the Pat Kenny radio show talking about the incident and TRUST. Later I was asked by An Gárda Síochána if they could use a tape of the interview for the training of guards. It sounds bizarre but to me this whole series of events was a sign to carry on – God's answer to my giving out to him!

Any time we have been looking for stuff at TRUST, we always say the person will come along if our work is to continue. Our wonderful nurse Geraldine is a case in point – truly an answer to prayer, even if it was not a very structured prayer. If you believe in what you do, you will get an inner strength from the Holy Spirit. My colleagues are out there now, washing feet and preparing the homeless for the day. We are here for that purpose. It is not easy and not everyone could do it, but neither could we do it without the prayers and practical help of so many people. We are in a very privileged position to make life a little easier for others and to make us thankful for what we have. The people we work with renew our faith in the human race. A listening ear is what many of them need – someone to hear their stories. The mystery of life is about our interactions with each other, for good or ill.

My faith mentors would have to include my own mother, who continues to inspire me with her independence and her deep faith. My friend Olivia Hughes was a great influence on my life. She was full of respect and care for everyone and did pioneering work in the ICA, the country markets and the League of the Blind. She was a doer who believed strongly in religion and prayer and who always encouraged us to question things. And I think it's very appropriate that we are doing this interview on St Brigid's Day. Brigid's life as a woman is an inspiration to us all. She challenged the thinking of her day, and her spirit is still alive and well.

I am in a confident space now, believing in what I believe in. You can get battered and bruised a lot in this work, but strength comes out of that. We are outsiders working with outsiders, but then wasn't Jesus an outsider too? I have great regard for missionaries in South America. They are showing that there is a God by what they do, and how they live, how they connect with the environment. I often think that old people who live up a country boreen are maybe more in touch with nature and the God who created this wonderful world than the rest of us. I have doubts about lots of things, but I don't waste my energy anymore in getting too annoyed at what I see happening in places in the name of religion. I am confident that I am guided by the Spirit and that people are praying for me. That gives me the strength to challenge bureaucracy or whatever gets in the way of our work. I know that if I speak out when necessary, tell the truth and do not lose touch with people who are suffering, I will always have support.

GORDON LINNEY

Gordon Linney was born in Dublin and educated at the High School, Rathgar. He was pursuing a successful career in banking until he felt the call to ministry and became a Church of Ireland rector. He served for seven years in Northern Ireland during the worst of the Troubles. Later he served in the Liberties of Dublin and in Glenageary in South Dublin, before being appointed Archdeacon of Dublin. Now retired, he is a frequent commentator on spiritual matters and writes a spiritual column in the Irish Times.

Our concept of God is way too small. When you look at what we have come to understand as the scale of the cosmos, the old Victorian idea of the gent with the long white beard sitting up in the sky is totally inadequate. One of the problems we have with it is that an awful lot of people are stuck there in their thinking. I believe in meaning and purpose. We see evidence of all that around us in the universe. I like the opening line of St John's Gospel: 'In the beginning was the Word.' It was a creative word, so I like to think of this God, this supreme being, as the great initiator, the great source of life and being. The theologian Paul Tillich described God as 'the ground of our being' and there is a great flexibility in that idea. It's a 'beyond' dimension, which is not only beyond our understanding but in many ways beyond our reach. We are always striving to know more fully who this supreme being is.

I suppose Jesus is the nearest we get to putting a face on God. I like the story of the little girl earnestly drawing a picture. When her mother enquires, the girl says she is drawing a picture of God. When the mother suggests that we don't know what God looks like, the girl replies, 'You will when I've finished my drawing!' In other words, there is an existential dimension to what we mean by God. We are always going to be looking for more. The Christian understanding is that we have been shown enough, but we will always be hungry for more.

I grew up in a faith-filled home, but it wasn't overtly so. We were not on our knees every day, but church-going was important. I have a memory of my mother reading a pink-covered, well-thumbed Bible every night. My father was a thinking Christian. When I was in my early teens and so arrogantly certain of my beliefs, he would question me on them. He was very quiet about his faith, but he would make you think. He clearly thought it was important for us to grow in that thinking environment. At school there was an attempt to awaken spiritual sensitivity or awareness in us, but I'm not sure how seriously we took it!

My avenue into the spiritual life was different. I was a choirboy in St Ann's, Dawson Street in Dublin and there we had a wonderful grounding in liturgy. I loved the Psalms and can still recite them in the old language, from before they were modernised. I was in a faith community which was disciplined and organised, and even though we messed around like all boys, I remember looking up to the people who were leading me, both clergy and community. I remember a particular curate, Horace McClelland, whom we absolutely loved. I wanted to be something like him, a person who was religious but who connected with me as a schoolboy. There were a number of people like that whom I met along the way, who encouraged me to think about ordination. The best known would be Archbishop George Otto Simms. He was chaplain in Kildare Place School when I attended. Anyone who came in contact with George Simms was touched and inspired by him. Having said that, I wasn't ordained until I was thirty years old, married with a child and in a promising career in the bank.

I look on faith as a journey of discovery. Faith implies doubt, there's no question about that. People who claim absolute certainty in faith are as bad as atheistic scientists who tell us there is no such thing as God. No serious scientist would make such a statement because they cannot prove it. It is equally true – and there will be religious people who won't like this – that we cannot prove the existence of God in a scientific way. I love the example of Abraham in the Old Testament: 'Abraham set out not knowing where he was going.' That is a powerful idea which should help other people who are struggling with faith, because that is the kind of journey that it is. For myself I have questions rather than doubts. My difficulties with religion have come more from institutional religion than from the core or heart of religion itself. Jesus Christ is so important in world history, so admired universally, way beyond Christianity. He represents something very, very special to us so I am very comfortable with the idea of belief in God and the unique way that Jesus Christ represents him in history.

My questioning would also relate to seeing some of the terrible sufferings that people have experienced in their lives. I lived through two phases of my own life where this happened. In 1962 I spent a year in a TB sanatorium. At the age of twenty-two I was dragged out of the circuit of life. I was very angry with that. Coming from a comfortable background into what was a rough environment, I found it very difficult to adjust. I was facing major surgery when Archbishop Simms came to visit me. I can still see him standing in the evening half-light, quoting Psalm 84 to me: 'Happy are those who when they walk in the arid valley, they make a spring of it and the pools are filled with water.' An extraordinary quotation which helped me come out of that experience much better after my initial wobble.

Then in 1987 there began a horrendous sequence of events for me. My brother died suddenly in September. My broken-hearted mother came to live with me and died in my house in January 1988. My sister died of cancer the following July. And in January 1990, my former curate, Stephen Hilliard, was killed in his rectory in Rathdrum, Co. Wicklow. Here was I preaching the resurrection and being sorely tested in believing there could be anything 'beyond' that would allow all this to happen. But again, I came out of that experience a better, wiser, stronger person. In my experience it is very often the people who suffer most who are the greatest witnesses to faith. If ever you want to see the Christian faith exemplified, you only have to look at [peace campaigner] Gordon Wilson, who always proclaimed himself to be 'an ordinary wee draper from Enniskillen'. Yet he had the extraordinary power to forgive great evil. I brought him to speak to young people in Glenageary and he cried as he told his story. In him I saw the power of the gospel for goodness and I thought – that is where I want to be, on that side of the debate.

When Maeve Binchy came out and said that she didn't believe, I thought to myself, 'Maeve, you've done wonders for religion, because it's all right not to believe!' The institutional churches don't really give that impression, because they are often more concerned with ownership and control. Historically they controlled education, health, etc. A lot of people were like the schoolboy who defined religion as believing what you know isn't true. At another level, there is the abuse of power and corruption. It has only been unveiled in recent times but for how long has it been going on? It was pure evil. When Jesus himself said if anyone should cause any of these little ones to stumble... it was probably his most severe judgement ever.

I am not looking at power in any denominational way, but it happens to be the most obvious example. When you look at the wealth of the Vatican and the pomp and ceremony of all the bishops and cardinals, where is Jesus Christ in all of this? He told us he would be found in the least of the poor. So yes, I have problems with the institutional Church. I think it's all right not to impose belief on someone who has been deeply hurt. There is such a thing as a non-conventional Christian. I buried many such people who never darkened the door of a church, but I know that in family and community they were generous, Christ-like people in the way they lived. So I'm not too hung up on the words 'I believe'. Jesus gave many examples of people who were outside the camp, as it were, like the Samaritan and the centurion.

I suppose my faith deepened in early adulthood, often through the example of the superb lives of 'ordinary' clergymen like Frank Alexander, my rector in Clondalkin. I admired him so much for the simplicity of his life, the sheer goodness of the man, his total dedication to service. I read *Naught For Your Comfort* by Trevor Huddleston. It was a damning indictment of the apartheid regime and a demand by him for action by the churches. It is set in the South Africa of the mid-1950s. He introduced me to something which would later become almost an obsession for me – connecting faith with life. For the first time I was seeing a Christian Church standing up strongly against evil and suffering for it. I later had the honour of meeting Archbishop Huddleston and also Archbishop Desmond Tutu – men who showed me that on the world stage the Christian gospel can be a transforming influence for good, as in the case of Gordon Wilson also. I would be very critical of the Church today for not connecting with everyday issues that concern people. When it comes to divorce, gay marriage or women priests, it's all hands to the pumps, but there are so many injustices in everyday life where we need the prophetic voice of the Church to connect our faith with action for social justice.

In the case of my own ministry, I served for seven years in Northern Ireland – during probably the worst seven years of violence there. I came back to Dublin to witness the poverty in the Liberties (there is a popular notion that there are no such things as poor Protestants). I loved the challenge of bringing respect to these people. They were so welcoming. I could leave my bike unattended while visiting them. After seven years I was sent to Glenageary in south Dublin. I was criticised there for my 'over-political' sermons. When I mentioned this to Desmond Tutu, he replied, 'Next time they say that, ask them what version of the Bible they are reading.' I speak equally well of Glenageary people, however. They became involved in issues at home – supporting the Simon Community and the TRUST charity for the homeless – and abroad, such as rebuilding a hospital in Uganda, which was an amazing success.

Prayer is obviously a big part of my life, but in an unconventional way. I have always been afraid of getting locked into the conventional 'shopping list' type of prayer. I have always felt that my everyday work had a dimension of prayer in it, 'the common things of life, its goings out and in', as the hymn puts it. I am also very disciplined, taking an hour's walk every morning – an opportunity for silence and reflection. I do of course engage in real intercessory prayer for people who have major problems, especially when I feel totally inadequate in dealing with those problems. In my own personal life, I have spent the last twenty years looking after my wife, who has Parkinson's disease. She is now in a nursing home, and it saddens me so much that she has little quality of life. That drives me to prayer, emotional prayer at times, for her peace of mind and that she will have enough understanding to know she is surrounded by love. I also pray with her. I put on CDs of hymns when I go in to feed her and she will sing along. I hope I am still connecting her with her faith in that way. Being with her is prayer, real presence.

I wouldn't be good at meditation but I do reflect a lot, especially when working in the garden. It is such an extraordinary place to learn things. I love music and when I listen to the magnificent works of Schubert, Mozart and Beethoven, I wonder what is the source of music in the human spirit. However you posit evolution as an explanation of the universe, if it's only a mechanistic thing you immediately devalue things like music, art, human love.

Death is beyond understanding and experience but it is not beyond expectation or hope, because at the heart of our faith is the sense that this experience of life is not the end. Nothing ever ceases to exist, so why would we not allow the possibility that the person continues after death in some form or other? I strongly believe that ultimately our lives are in the embrace of a loving Creator and within that dimension we survive in some way. We would be very foolish to try and over-define what that would be. Heaven for me is intimacy with God. St Paul says, 'We know in part, we prophecy in part, then shall we know.' In a way he too is acknowledging doubt – the possibility that he could be wrong. I always say a bishop's crozier is really a question mark! On the contrary, hell to me would be separation from God. The fire and brimstone stuff came out of the Jewish experience of terrible suffering. Jesus said the kingdom of heaven is within you *now*, not down the road.

If I could have accompanied Jesus in his lifetime, I would love to have seen him lose his temper and clear the temple. It runs counter to the 'gentle Jesus, meek and mild' image, which he never was. He was passionate about social justice and when he came up against the hypocrisy of the institution and the racket of the chief priests fixing the exchange rates – such a contemporary issue – he demonstrated a righteous anger, which is part of the Christian mission.

My image of the Christian Church is expressed in a line from the *Book of Common Prayer*, which at the end of the Eucharist refers to the Church as 'the blessed company of all faithful people'. I love that concept, because to me the Church is like a mosaic, made up of pieces of all shapes, sizes, angles and colours. That is the glorious diversity of the community travelling this faith journey, not knowing where we are going, like Abraham. I love that dimension of mystery in our religious life, because it means I am going to be surprised.

JOHN LONERGAN

John Lonergan is a native of Bansha, Co. Tipperary. He joined the prison service, initially in Limerick and later served in Loughan House, Cavan; in Shanganagh Castle, Co. Dublin; in Portlaoise; and in Mountjoy Prison, Dublin, where he rose to the rank of governor. His twenty-four years' tenure as governor was marked by initiative, wisdom, humanity and compassion. Now retired after forty-two years in the service, he is much in demand as a speaker and commentator. He has presented a television series on marginalised youth, and his autobiography, The Governor: The Life and Times of the Man Who Ran Mountjoy *(2011), received wide acclaim for its honesty and insight.*

My personal belief centres on the spirit or, if you like, the soul. Each of us has a spirit and that spirit is a very important element of my life. Obviously, I hope against hope that there is something more to life than just living it, even though 'living it' is a central tenet of my belief. I don't honestly believe that at the end of time we will all rise up and be visible in body, but I do believe the spirit part of us will continue and live on. I accept that many people have a very strong belief and have no reservations at all about their faith or any element of it. I would struggle with some of those elements because of my own life experience and because, quite frankly, some of it doesn't seem very logical. I recognise that much of what we are asked to believe is mystery, but I suppose life itself would be very depressing if there was nothing to it other than mere existence and then a blank at the end.

I grew up in the rural Ireland of the 1950s, in a little place called Bansha in County Tipperary, and I would obviously have been influenced in terms of belief by the culture of that time, by my parents, by the local community and of course by the Catholic

Church, which exerted a powerful control on all our lives. Every member of that Church went to Mass and the Sacraments. It would be most unusual not to attend Sunday Mass. It would be noticed and talked about. The annual mission and the stations were major events in our lives. I spent a number of years as an altar boy. At home we had the family rosary every night, orchestrated by my mother.

Fear was a huge part of the philosophy of the Catholic Church. If you didn't do A, B and C you were ruined, damned forever. We were innocent and accepted that. The world was a very distant place. Our only links with it were the radio and the *Clonmel Nationalist*. My parents, my neighbours, never questioned any aspect of their faith. It was a very rigid and domineering system. For young people today, with so much information instantly available and so much contact with the world, it is a completely different situation.

Personally, I only began to question the world and my beliefs when I entered the prison system at the age of twenty. I very quickly became aware of inequality, pain, suffering, injustice. How and why did this happen? How could 'caring' people be responsible for starving children or domestic violence? I was looking out for examples of Christian philosophy, the principles of forgiveness especially, kindness and generosity. The necessity to forgive was for me the hub of Christianity. The Church as an institution was not always to the forefront in that regard. How good were Church leaders at forgiving? I felt that in some cases they failed miserably. I still struggle with that.

In my search for forgiveness and understanding, Jesus became closer to me than a 'God' figure – Jesus the man. I can identify so much with a lot of the stuff attributed to Jesus. I could not find any better philosophy for living, for really participating in life. The principles of Jesus' example will stand up in any context. The challenge for me is to live those principles. If you don't live it, there is no point in going through the cosmetics of it. The challenge for me, for all of us, is to put forgiveness, compassion and mercy into practice day by day. Attending Mass and following rituals is the easy part; the hard part is to live it. A lot of people don't, and I would include some Church leaders here. When priests who were convicted of abuse ended up in prison they were often totally disowned by society. Yes, they did horrible things but for me the person of each priest was still there. They sinned but where do we stand?

There is no need to preach your virtues if you live by them. The 'cosmetics' of one's faith might seem a strong word, but if you go to Mass and Communion every day and then come out and do the opposite of what is required of you as a Christian – cheat, injure, rob from your neighbour – then to me what you are doing is very cosmetic indeed. I know a parish priest who moved on a family of travellers who had lodged themselves in the church car park. He did this under pressure from parishioners. To me that was totally incompatible with Christianity. Those people who attended Mass and then went round to pressurise the priest do not understand the meaning of living a Christian life. The gospels for me are a way of living life rather than going through the motions.

Prayer, in the sense of formal prayer, would not be a central part of my life. When I go to Mass or funerals I participate of course, but I'm not a daily praying person. I am more given to reflection, to challenging and questioning, seeing what is happening, why it is happening and how it might be prevented. So many of the issues in prison are due to neglect in the early years – children at huge risk and families struggling way beyond their competency. That is what motivated me to be reflective. Where is all this trouble coming from? How can I understand it? Is this just or fair? If not, why is that the case? I have to say that very often it is us – we Christians have caused and inflicted an awful lot of suffering on others. I am reminded of Gandhi's words, 'I like your Christ, I do not like your Christians.'

Throughout my forty-two years in the prison service, my beliefs were very central to my work. There were two approaches I could have taken: either to be a hardline authoritarian, a disciplinarian, a control freak, or to be a Christian who sees prisoners as human beings who should be treated with respect. One of my great mentors in this regard was my colleague, Dick Crowe, who instigated the introduction of Open Centres in the 1970s. He spoke to us about putting Christianity into practice. If you really want to do that, there is no better place to do it than in working with young offenders. These are young people who have potential, with long lives ahead of them. They can be redirected with care and humanity to a more meaningful, positive lifestyle. You can do this by treating them with kindness and respect rather than seeing their behaviour as an integral part of them as human beings. Young offenders, in my experience, respond far more genuinely to 'soft' skills than a harsh, physical approach, and if they start on that journey, they are far more likely to stay the course.

Another great mentor of mine was the parish priest of Bansha when I was a child – Canon Hayes, who founded *Muintir na Tíre* [a national voluntary organisation dedicated to promoting the process of community development]. I still remember his sermons. The whole parish became involved in what he believed in – a community as a social mix of equals. This may seem normal now, but seventy years ago it was revolutionary. All his philosophical stuff about the danger of materialism, the need for people to be in contact, to share their time and gifts, to help the struggling, all of that left a mark on me and very much influenced me in my work.

My parents also influenced me greatly. My mother was a strong believer in basic Christianity – being welcoming, sharing and being absolutely honest. That was the way of life they practised and it was quite typical of her generation. Some might see it as a naive and simple approach to life but I think that it is to our cost that we have lost much of that simplicity. The gospels often refer to the need for living simple lives and I am convinced that the more simple and humble your life, the more you will enjoy it. The Celtic Tiger period was the best example of how far we have moved from the simple life. It was a competition to get to the top. Now it is a race to the bottom. We need to find a balance between those extremes. Yes, we need a house, food, clothes, facilities, but what we don't need is all the 'trimmings' of the Tiger period.

Another great influence in my life is Jean Vanier, founder of the L'Arche organisation, which provides community living for the disabled and the broken in our society. Vanier gave up his comfortable life to seek out and befriend the marginalised and friendless. He is the true definition of a 'walking saint', simply because he practises what he preaches, recognising that 'man's most primal cry is to be loved'. I had the great honour of sharing a weekend with him in Derry some years ago. His words remain with me: 'To listen another human being into a condition of disclosure is the greatest service you can bestow on a fellow human being.'

One of the biggest scourges in modern Ireland is loneliness and disconnection. There never was a perfect era. There never were the 'good old days'. There was always a mix of good and bad. Today technology and travel are wonderful but there are many negatives in modern life. One of the pluses in the old days was far better connection to community. We visited and were visited. We had someone to listen. Today so many people have no one to talk to and are dismissed. They are never consulted or involved in decision making. It is little wonder many of them get into trouble. Listening is a gift we can all employ. But it takes one thing – time – and often we are not prepared to give that time. There is a great culture of self-interest nowadays. We can blame the government and various institutions for loneliness but it is not all their fault. We need balance in our own lives. Our education system must also take some of the blame. It tends to be uni-directional: how to make a living. The economy is there to serve people, not the other way around.

I think if I had lived in the time of Jesus we would have got on well together! I couldn't disagree with what he said and did. It was all about treating people properly, showing forgiveness, welcoming the prodigal. That is very powerful for me. My problem is that a lot of what Jesus stood for I cannot see being implemented today. This creates doubts for me. How can you have such a powerful philosophy, so soundly based, and yet it is a million miles away from how we operate in many instances? I am an optimist by nature – nothing is unsolvable. Change is a slow process; you can't force it and you would be a fool to try. The only way is to nurture and encourage, to keep raising awareness. I spoke recently to young people at the Dundalk Family Resource Centre. I told them there is no reason to have a blank CV even if you have no job. Your CV should be full of things you are doing for your community – visiting an old person, helping in a youth club. Fill your CV by doing a few positive things every day rather than sitting at home.

The same goes for anyone aspiring to be a Christian. You will need lots of stuff on your CV to prove it. On the Last Day you will get a call if you have a CV. If not, you will be challenged to justify your claim to be a Christian. And after that? I don't know. I hope, for example, my mother's spirit is well, that she is 'someplace' and that her life didn't disappear when she died. Twenty-one years after her death, I still cannot comprehend the afterlife. I am optimistic there is something but I have no evidence. There should be a place for the Jean Vaniers, the Canon Hayes's, who put themselves last in the service of others. And indeed for the many 'ordinary' people I met in my work, who treat the most alienated in our society with respect. For me, they equal those who lived long ago who are now regarded to be saints. As for the 'other direction', I have no belief in hell. I have a lot of difficulty with the notion that if you do A you will be rewarded, whereas if you do B there will be ruination in fire awaiting you. I can't believe that. We should be living the Christian life anyway, not simply for a promised reward at the end. We have fantastic people in Ireland giving of themselves, doing amazing work, truly living a philosophy of Christianity. We need a greater sense of community and belonging, just like Canon Hayes promoted seventy years ago.

If someone told me now that there is nothing at the end of life, it wouldn't change anything for me. I would still believe in a philosophy of Christianity. Death doesn't bother me. I am totally relaxed with the notion that from the day you are born the only next inevitable thing is death. So you must make the best of the period in between. Life is your greatest gift, so enjoy it and do the best you can with it. If you can do good, do good. If you cannot, do nothing! My belief is best summed up in the Book of Micah: 'Act justly, love tenderly, walk humbly with your God.'

DAVID NORRIS

David Norris was born in the former Belgian Congo but came to Ireland at an early age. He was educated at St Andrew's College, The High School and Trinity College Dublin, where he later became a senior lecturer from 1968–96. Member of Seanad Éireann, upper house of Dáil Eireann, since 1987. He was the first openly gay person elected to public office in Ireland and won the case for the decriminalisation in Ireland of homosexual acts at the European Court of Human Rights in 1985. He is also a Joycean scholar who has lectured and written extensively on the author. He was a candidate for the presidency of Ireland in 2011 and his autobiography, A Kick Against the Pricks, *was published by Transworld in 2012.*

I believe in God, in Jesus Christ, in an absolutely committed way – but I would always retain the 'principle of positive doubt'. We cannot say we know the nature of God or his existence in the same way that we know the physical world, which we discern by our senses. The principle of positive doubt is good because it shows you have arrived at something as a result of a journey and you have decided that your belief is correct on the balance of evidence and tradition. That principle prevents arrogance, which sadly is a trait to be found in many of the traditional religions. When I say the Creed, I leave some things out. I do not believe in the resurrection of the body, but I believe in the resurrection of the dead – and I say that.

There are so many ways to define God. Some people find it difficult to believe in God because they cannot believe in the Victorian construct of the God with which I was brought up – a sort of benign bearded Santa Claus, sitting on a cloud. I remember the controversy that John Robinson caused with his book *Honest to God*, when he uprooted that Victorian image. Like many people, I initially felt devastated and disturbed, but to be disturbed is good. I see 'God' now as a presence, but that Santa Claus image lingered for a time from my childhood days, when we attended St Mary's church in Anglesea Road, Dublin. When Communion started, we little ones were taken into the vestry for Bible class. This was lovely. You got a stamp every time you attended. When you had a book full of stamps, you got a Bible or a prayer book. In those books, God was portrayed as a comforting father figure, but that was a long time ago.

I was always very comfortable going to church. My family were a strong influence on my faith formation. My grandmother was not an overtly pious woman, but she was a very good person. She read the Bible constantly and she sang me to sleep with hymns. I loved her. She died when I was eleven and a few weeks later I woke to find her standing at my bed for a full minute. For my mother, going to church was a treat – if you were naughty, you were not brought to church! I have only a few memories of my father, who died when I was five. On wet Sundays we read *Pilgrim's Progress* or were brought for an 'improving walk' by my aunt. She would tell me the names of trees and birds (referring to Aunt Amy's bird book). I loved being with her. All those wonders of nature clearly provided a rhythm and a connection with the pattern of life. I find it difficult to believe that creation was accidental. For me it is easier to believe in God – a spirit of goodness – and in the historical figure of Jesus Christ whose life still affects people for good, than in black holes, dark matter, parallel universes, etc. This is my faith. The gospel means 'good news' and I obviously want to spread it, but if you have bad news *à la* Richard Dawkins, the decent thing would be to keep it to yourself!

My mother died when I was twenty-one. I found her dead in bed just after Christmas. It was my first experience of dealing personally with death and it was a horrible experience. It destroyed my sense of reality. This world could not be real if someone I loved so much is gone. Faith seemed meaningless then. It made me terrified of my own death. It was quite a wobble, but as the years went by I gradually recovered my belief and I continued going to church.

Prayer was a big part of my childhood. We had to go on our knees and pray each morning. My mother would say the Collects and grew to love them. I understand the centrality of the rosary for Roman Catholics and would have the same love for the Collects. In fact, I have adapted parts of the rosary for myself. When I take Communion on Sundays, I say, 'Jesus be with me now and at the hour of my death.' And I believe he will be with me and so my faith grows stronger. My prayers generally are for others, not for myself. I have St Patrick's Cathedral practically burned to the ground with all the candles I have lit over the years. I don't know if they have any impact but they remind me to think of people and make contact with them. My prayers are not always petitionary. Some of my prayers are reflections on how wonderful life is and how glorious it is to be alive. Gratitude should also be a major part of prayer. When I see a young couple holding hands in the street, I say, 'God bless you ... I wish you well.' That's another kind of prayer. I pray whenever I feel like it. I wouldn't be one for going on my knees at the end of the bed! I actually tried to get prayer banned in the Senate. I thought it was just being spouted out for the sake of formality. Why should acts of parliament derive from Jesus, just because I believe in him? What about other faiths?

Faith may be a gift, but it needs to be worked at. I feel so terribly sad that religious practices have collapsed in this country for reasons that are irrelevant. The abuse scandals were horrendous but that was not a reason for not believing in Christ or in the values of Christianity. We heard so many amateur theologians being judgemental and hypocritical. I am reminded of the Scripture, 'Though I speak with the tongues of men and angels and do not have charity, I have become as sounding brass or a tinkling cymbal.' There are, to my mind, an awful lot of cymbals tinkling. People seem to be abandoning the Church for reasons not directly connected to the real core of religion.

I love the discipline of going to church. I never miss a Sunday simply because I love it and find it refreshing. I feel the presence of God directly in the Communion service. The moment of Consecration is mystical and beautiful, and at the moment of taking Communion I feel in touch with the whole mystical world of people who are alive, yet to come and departed. I am nourished by that and equally by the sermons, psalms and readings, which are extraordinarily relevant to our lives, if we but listen to them. They kept me going through the enduring misery of media attacks during my candidacy in the presidential election.

I totally accept that much of what we believe is mystery. I leave mystery to Queen Elizabeth I – she solves it beautifully in her little quatrain:

His the lips that spake it
His the hands that break it
Whatsoe'er that doth make it
For that shall I take it.

Why should we waste so much time trying to 'understand' the mystery of transubstantiation? People have been murdered all over Europe because of it. It flies against reason that we don't see any physical change in the bread and wine. I leave that to Elizabeth. I cannot know what is outside my knowledge. People are individuals, bringing their own personality to the rituals of the Church and those rituals help them. Places like Knock, Lourdes and Medjugorje are intensely holy places but I personally don't believe that the Blessed Virgin ever went near them. To me they are sanctified by the faith of the people who went there, by comradeship, by human suffering, by belief in God. Why would the Blessed Virgin only land in those places? Why not land in Dr Paisley's pulpit or in front of the Ayatollah?

The Holy Spirit is rather indefinable to me but I believe in it because this Spirit resides within us all. The only physical image of God that I have is of Jesus Christ – not the popular blond, blue-eyed man we often see pictured, but rather the kind of person I would see in a carpenter's shop when I lived in Israel. I see him as a young Semitic man. I know the gospel records are not contemporaneous, but I have no doubt that he was a historical figure. I would love to have been with him at the Last Supper – just to be party to the continuation of the Jewish Friday ritual and to witness the beginning of Mass and Communion as we know them.

Saint Paul has mediated a lot of the history of the early Church, but the wisdom, love, generosity and charity of Jesus and the beauty of his spirit is Godlike. That Spirit communicates itself to me, so I believe that when I die I will be taken in his arms and brought to heaven. I don't believe in hell. It's a contradiction. It just cannot exist. How could an all-wise, all-merciful God sentence his creatures to an eternity of torment, misery and suffering? I think Hitler's hell, for example, will be to realise the evil he did. He won't be a happy bunny, I would say! I cannot believe in a physical devil but I do believe there is a constant battle between good and evil, between creativity and destruction, between happiness and self-induced misery. My concept of heaven, on the other hand, is just consciousness, happiness, being in the presence of God.

I have no fear of death but who is to say that at the moment of death I won't be screaming 'I'm terrified!' I just don't know. I think death is (or should be) gentle. There are three things I fear at the point of death: agonising pain, nausea and struggling for breath. I hope I stay conscious for as long as possible, because I want to experience dying as a wonderful adventure. I have my burial planned – in a wicker basket under a tree in Roskelton in County Laois. The worms can then feed away on me – why not?

I was brought up with the belief that religion is a private thing. My relationship with God is a very intimate thing so I have a certain resistance to trying to spread my views around, but I have to overcome that to share them with those who want to share them. That is why I have organised my own funeral the way I have done. There will be lots of fun but I will also have the last word – a speech from the box which I hope will encourage people.

I am very encouraged by the emergence of Pope Francis. I had an awful feeling when his predecessor was elected, but when Francis was elected I immediately felt that this was a reincarnation of the wonderful John XXIII. That moment of silence when he came on the balcony and asked a million people to pray with him! Silence! That is the most wonderful moral authority; so much more important than all the talk of the magisterium of the Church, that imperial system which lacks the humility of Christ. Then the new pope crowned it all by taking the name of Francis, thus identifying himself with the poor. I look forward to good things.

My faith is central to my life and my work. It sustains me, particularly now when I am fighting cancer. I had a major operation to separate and save an artery from the tumour that had enveloped it. I hate the pain involved. It distorts time. I had one night of the most violent agony which I tried to stifle before I had to give in and go to hospital. Even in hospital you may have to wait two or three minutes for the morphine to be signed for by the doctor, but that feels like centuries when you are holding on to the sides of the bed in pain. Yet all these things are temporal. We have at best a lifespan of a hundred years. In the infinity of time, that is nothing. The suffering can be appalling, but how can I complain when I think of others like the EB [Epidermolysis Bullosa] children, whose skin is so fragile from the moment of birth that their flesh is raw. But even that doesn't last forever. That's why death is wonderful. I hope I can die serenely like my great friend from my schooldays, who died from cancer but maintained his Christian faith through all the pain and indignity. I don't like the idea of miracles. Why should I get one in preference to, say, that wonderful young man from Tralee, Dónal Walsh, who had a whole life of maybe sixty or seventy years ahead of him? What might he have contributed over a full lifespan? For me to have a 'miraculous' cure just wouldn't be fair.

Who has inspired me? While he wasn't a believer, Noel Browne was a good, good man. Victor Griffin, the former Dean of St Patrick's, is another man I admire, and of course his predecessor a few centuries back, Jonathan Swift. I love his earthiness and his superb satires, that savage indignation with which he looked on injustice. I love Archbishop Tutu as someone who can laugh and be human, be fallible and warm. And of course Pope John XXIII, who shook up the slowness of the Vatican to change. He is unquestionably a saint. The beautiful music of Mozart, Schubert, Bach, Haydn – especially those pieces which are part of church worship – lifts me up.

A lot of life depends on how you approach it. I have an incurably optimistic nature. I am happy wherever I am. Through all my life, especially through all my difficulties, my faith has sustained me. That is why I would like to make my experience available to anyone who might have the germ of faith within them, because it could sustain them. Church-going is so important in my life. It grows on me and I continue to absorb the message and wisdom it imparts. The other thing that sustains me is the sheer goodness and affection of people. When news of my illness became public, I was hit by a tsunami of cards, Mass bouquets, prayers and candle offerings. They have lifted me so much. No one exudes goodness more than the Pro-Cathedral twins – Gin and Tonic (that's how they are known!). They think and talk as one. They are so good and happy and full of positive energy. Like the Poor Clares, their vocation is to pray and they pray for me and many others. They are so saintly and life-enhancing. They certainly enhance my life, God bless them.

I believe in an afterlife. I don't know how it will be but to my mind it's not possible to say that consciousness dies completely. I am sure people would want to see their loved ones as they knew them, but I don't know. Although I loved my granny, I'm not going to queue up to see her – it would be such a big queue! I believe we will be re-absorbed into a kind of consciousness. I feel my mother and my aunt around the place, speaking through me. I just don't know. We'll see.

BREDA O'BRIEN

Breda O'Brien is a native of County Waterford and was educated at the Convent of Mercy, Dungarvan, and Mater Dei Institute, Dublin. She began her career as a teacher of religion in Dublin, then worked as a video producer in the Catholic Communications Centre, Dublin, and as a researcher for RTÉ, before returning to teaching. She is founder of Feminists for Life, a leader in the pro-life movement, and a patron of the Iona Institute, a conservative Catholic lobby group and think-tank. A regular commentator on religious affairs on radio and television, she also writes a weekly column in the Irish Times.

The older I get the more I realise how ill-fitted I am to know God. I have a greater sense of my own tininess and my inability to comprehend anything as awe-inspiring as the idea of God. Growing up in the Christian tradition, I always had a huge love for Jesus the man. Even at times when my faith in Jesus the Christ dimmed, I always had a great love for Jesus the man. The older I get, the more I see myself as opening out to what God wants rather than my directing him to what he should be doing with the world. That contemplative direction has grown in my life.

I grew up in a very traditional Catholic household. My parents were daily Mass-goers, the rosary was a nightly ritual. My father gave many years to the Society of St Vincent de Paul. My mother was a Child of Mary. All of that didn't necessarily take with everyone in the family, but it was definitely an influence. We were a family of four, and as we got bigger and bolder, my mother's ambitions became more modest – we went from the full rosary to a single decade! We lived on a farm beside the sea in Waterford. Mine was a lonely childhood in ways – there were not many children of my age around and there were big gaps on either side of me in my own family, so I was a solitary child who loved reading. All of those factors nurtured a reflective spirit in me, not about spiritual things, just a habit of thinking.

After school I went to the Mater Dei Institute in Dublin to study Theology, Education and English. I was a naive seventeen-year-old who only opted for Mater Dei because they were nice to me at the interview. It was a tiny college of two hundred students but it was a good time for me. They had a very good theology department, but I really found nurture in the English department, where they had brilliant lecturers, especially John Devitt. His lectures in an old prefab are my warmest memories of Mater Dei. Patrick Kavanagh's poetry, the epiphanies he had on the wonders of everyday things, was a huge influence on me. Poetry can condense ideas so well. As the feminist theologian Dorothee Sölle puts it, poetry and prayer connect us to our hopes.

I became a teacher and as a busy twenty-something, my faith drifted somewhat. I was certainly not a staunch believer. I then met my husband Brendan at Teach Bhríde in Tullow, a Christian house of welcome for young people. I think we all come to God through some kind of experience of love, and the essence of Brendan is loyalty and love. His faith has always been enormously important to him in a very practical way. My faith was seriously tested when I lost a baby through miscarriage. I felt none of that made sense. How could a loving God let a tiny innocent baby die in its mother's supposedly safe womb? For months and months I felt utter bleakness. What was it all for? Was all this faith stuff a myth? Eventually I found myself slowly, slowly coming back. There was no great moment of revelation. I suppose whatever faith was there was deeply grounded and also just being around Brendan brought light and warmth back. He refused to be thrown by the fact that the Catholic he married was now an atheist. I consider myself a fairly shallow Catholic in many ways, given the background I had. I am a distractable person – I feel I haven't plumbed the depths I could have.

I feel privileged in that every part of my life has been folded into every other part. Even in writing for the *Irish Times*, there is a chance to reflect on things I am interested in, but in all sincerity I can skitter along on the surface like a pond skater. I wouldn't really consider myself great shakes as a believer or as an example to others. I am profoundly aware of my own failings and superficiality in many ways, but my faith is central to my life. For all that, I don't pray as regularly as I would like to and I don't put the effort into reading scriptures that I would like to. I do make attempts from time to time to find some kind of spiritual direction. Only recently we have started taking three minutes' silence after a family meal, followed by a short scripture reading. I find that very helpful. At various stages I tried contemplative prayer and failed miserably. If it was a set of copies that needed correction or an *Irish Times* deadline, however, I would not be found wanting. If my spiritual life is as important as I keep saying it is, I would be finding more time to put into it. That annoys me about myself. I know it sounds pious, but sometimes your life is your prayer. If I am with a child who is in difficulty and there is a moment of silence, that's a very sacred moment because it is rare for them to be in silence with someone just accepting them and it is rare for me to have that moment of silence. I feel I am touching the hem of the garment of someone who really cares.

Teaching religion is very difficult. Without my own faith I don't think I could keep going, because I belong in the Book of Heroic Failures when it comes to teaching religion. There are huge cultural gaps to be overcome. Young people are losing vocabulary, concepts, time – it is both fascinating and scary to watch. If I do meditation or prayer with the students, they lap it up, but their faith has become very individualised. They don't have a great sense of community. That to me is a massive part of my faith – that I belong to an imperfect, messy, human community – and it is through that community that God speaks to me. That kind of language would be alien to my students. They aren't reading as much anymore and they have difficulty with concepts that writers like Kavanagh or Gerard Manley Hopkins might use. In a culture where distractability is a virtue, today's students are constantly wired to something. Technology is wonderful – I personally couldn't live without the internet – but it means the ability to come down into yourself, be quiet, reflect, is missing. Many of the young people are scared of silence, of what they will find in themselves if they are quiet. There was a structure in society that once supported that, but that can no longer be taken for granted. My idea of heaven would be to sit quietly in Ballyvooney Cove, Co. Waterford, looking out at the waves and spend an hour or two just being there.

I am an absolute believer in mystery, even if my brain isn't big enough for concepts like the Trinity or transubstantiation. I equally believe in the miracle of everyday life – the fact that two people can meet, marry, drive each other mad and still grow, that a child can be born. Because of my love for literature, I know that the world is so much bigger than my narrow horizon. I accept that the brain cannot understand transubstantiation, but I am enormously glad that it exists and that I have the privilege to be part of it. I was recently reading a blog, These Stone Walls, of a priest who claims he was falsely accused of child abuse. His absolute love for the Eucharist is stunning. When he realised the chaplain in prison had the Eucharist, there were tears in his eyes. I don't have that depth of faith or reverence, but I went to Mass on the following Sunday with a sense of privilege. You cannot take the Eucharist for granted. If you dismiss it as some kind of medieval nonsense, it is like a dulling of your senses. The Mass is important to me on all sorts of levels: as a vehicle to help to raise my children in faith; as a community event, where I can meet others for whom it is equally important. The Mass is just important in itself, when I feel my own littleness and inability to have more regard for it than I actually do. Last year's Eucharistic

Congress helped me a lot. To see people from all over the world with such reverence for the central part of all our lives was an amazing experience.

I am a hopeful person but there is a lot in everyone's world that can knock your sense of hope. I find, for example, the rise of atomised individualism very distressing because *ar scáth a chéile a mhaireann na daoine* (people live in each other's shadows). We need each other. The narrowing down in the moral field to consent or choice worries me. The young people I teach are wonderful but they will constantly say, 'It was his choice' or 'You cannot knock somebody's choice'. The concept that there can be bad choices as well as good is disappearing. If someone makes a choice, they have to live with it, it seems. That shows a lack of compassion. As I grow older I am more aware of the sweep of history – this is just a moment in time. Values that seem to be gone forever can be recovered. I am hopeful of that. I am not being nostalgic for a lost age. There never was a utopia. Nostalgia can be very dangerous. There are many good things about the current generation. They are much more in touch with their emotions and much more able to articulate what they feel – something I didn't have, growing up. What we have lost from our parents' generation is a sense of responsibility to the broader community. My dad died at the age of ninety-three but so many of his neighbours said to me, 'He was a quiet fellow, but if you were in trouble, he would turn up.' Society today doesn't reward or reinforce those values, which is very foolish for the long-term survival of the race or the planet.

Raising my children in faith is an important part of my faith. I would love them to have contact with what I consider the Ultimate Reality and for them to be shaped by that. For me it's like a true north. If you could orient your life towards this, it will always draw you beyond what you want to be yourself, will always cause you to look towards other people and will feed your soul and imagination. I want them to have that, but I know I have no control – nor should I have – over whether they will accept that or not. If they all grow up to be card-carrying atheists, I would still love them to pieces, but I do feel the responsibility of helping them to have that true north in their lives and then it's up to them to take it or leave it. And we do have very interesting conversations in our house.

I have great regard for Dorothy Day as a faith mentor, even if I am nine million miles away from what she achieved – her ability to be radical and yet to be utterly immersed in her faith. She had a difficult life, having a relationship and a child which she had to give up when she began to draw closer to the Catholic message. She had a great collaborator in Peter Maurin and chose the radical option of poverty and to be really close to people on the margins – very difficult people to be around. It was all part of her spirituality. Ironically, although they seemed to be the antithesis of each other, she had great devotion to Thérèse of Lisieux. I grew up with a syrupy notion of Thérèse as a smiling woman with an armful of roses, but there is immense strength in her. Dorothy Day wrote a book simply called *Thérèse*, in which she said that when she looked at the world and all its difficulties, and then noted the apathy and lack of care about these things, the more convinced she was of the need to return to the 'little way' of Thérèse. I found that very helpful. Just keep putting one foot in front of the other. Do what is put in front of you at the time. Try not to moan or have too big an ego. Just get on with it and put it in the hands of God.

I grew up at a time when the role of Mary was de-emphasised, but I have come back to her in more recent times – not the plaster saint in blue; that means nothing to me. The centrality of the feminine in the Catholic tradition is very warming and sustaining to me. There is a song, *A Mhuire Mháthair*, which says '*Is tusa mo mháthair is Máthair Dé*' (You are my mother and God's mother too). That moves me enormously. The notion of a young woman who could face stoning because of being pregnant outside marriage means a great deal to me and I love the few words we have from her in scripture, especially the Magnificat.

If I could have accompanied Jesus for one day, I think it would be the day he called the children to him. That was so different to the culture of the time: 'The disciples rebuked them, but Jesus said "Let the children come to me ... for the kingdom of heaven belongs to such as these"', i.e. the idea of being little and vulnerable should be valued. Life is not about power or ego. We need to be in relationship with each other and care for each other. I believe intergenerational relationships are hugely important – whether child to parent or parent to their parents. So it would have been very moving to have been with Jesus when he promoted that care and solidarity.

As an institution, the Church has had me bordering on clinical depression at times! My son, who is twenty, has never known a time when the Church was held in high regard. There has been a period of stasis and even stagnation. We are still waiting for a model of Church where lay people are central. We have lost an everyday spirituality. I have brought my students to the mosque, where they met devout Muslims and learned how they pray often and try to remain in constant awareness of God. The students were taken aback because they haven't really experienced that in their own everyday life – it's more a once-a-week thing. We are still looking to the bishops for leadership, but there is not enough leadership happening there. Because I write a column in the *Irish Times*, there is notion that I have the ear of people in power in the Church. That is so far from the truth as to be farcical. In a sense, there is no centre of power in that way – many of the bishops are ageing, although there are individuals who have passion and commitment. For a long time I wondered, is there no one who will give us a lead, take a prophetic stance? To my amazement, through the courageous and unprecedented step that Pope Benedict took in standing down, we have a dynamic and prophetic leader in Francis. It won't be enough, of course, because the challenge comes to everyone of us to try and make our faith real in our lives, but it is the most wonderful boost.

Overall I am highly dissatisfied with my own commitment to my faith. I feel a great sense of inadequacy in that regard, but I also feel that God laughs at me a lot. I read a great line once: the gap between your best self and your worst from God's perspective is so tiny as to be laughable. We think we could be this great and wonderful thing, but from the perspective of an omnipotent God our best self might be no great shakes! What I would like to incorporate in my life is more day-to-day trust, more ability to step back and put my ego aside, to put myself more into the moment with faith, hope and love. I am blessed in having friends in whom I have seen that develop – one in particular who was quite acerbic in his younger days but is now retired and mellowed, because of the amount of time he spent praying and living out his life. That is my aspiration but I am nowhere near achieving it.

MARY O'HARA

Mary O'Hara was born in Sligo and educated by the Dominican Sisters in Sion Hill, Dublin. She became a proficient singer and harpist. She married the American poet, Richard Selig, but fifteen months later he died from Hodgkin's disease. She then entered the monastic life, joining the Benedictine Sisters in Stanbrook, England. After a number of contented years there, she was advised on medical grounds to leave the monastic life. She resumed her singing career and became an international star. She later met a former missionary, Pat O'Toole, and they married in 1985. They spent six years in Africa where Pat was teaching. They now live on Inis Mór, Aran Islands. She has written two acclaimed autobiographies, The Scent of the Roses *(1980) and* Travels With My Harp *(2012).*

I have a strong faith but it is something I have to work at to keep it strong. I accept the Apostles' Creed in its entirety. I was born into the Catholic faith in Sligo and grew up in that culture. There was never any questioning of the faith at school but I was grounded in it in a very good sense. My father was a civil engineer who later joined the British Army. The practice of religion was strong but my parents had an unsatisfactory marriage. There was a lot of tension and unhappiness. Sometimes in the midst of all that, you would wonder why they said the rosary, but they did! I suppose each of us gets the amount of light we really need.

My mother was musical and taught me lots of songs as a small child. At school my voice was noticed and I was entered by my teachers to compete in various *feiseanna*. I used to dread Easter when the *feiseanna* came around. I hated the nervousness of performing but I managed to win various awards. I was sent to boarding school in Sion Hill, Dublin, where I met my singing teacher, Sister Angela Walsh, and was introduced to the harp, which would eventually launch me on an international career as a singer and harpist. As regards my faith at that time, it was just part of the culture. I would never try to analyse or wonder why I believed what I believed. All this would change when I met Richard.

Richard Selig was a poet from the USA who was studying as a Rhodes Scholar in Oxford. He had seen me singing in Dublin and insisted on inviting me out on a date. I was young – barely out of my teens – and at a very formative part of my life. He was in his mid-twenties and profoundly talented. I was very flattered. Had he not been attracted to me and had he not pursued me, I would certainly not have pursued him because I would have thought I hadn't a chance. He had studied at the Catholic University in Washington but he was not a believer, in the sense that he did not have any creed nor did he have a religious family background. He was a searcher and a poet. He had studied comparative religion in Washington and certainly knew more about the Catholic Church, its history and doctrine, than I who had grown up in that faith. He was quite rooted in God – he once told me he was 'fascinated by Christ'. He had enormous integrity and instinctively knew right from wrong. He was not in any way a puritan – far from it. We fell in love and he was the first great influence on me. He caused me to examine what I believed in because he felt I should be committed to that belief. He instigated a spirit of enquiry within me. We became completely one and when he proposed to me one morning in Oxford I immediately said yes.

Richard had to undergo 'instruction' in the Catholic faith as part of our preparation for marriage. He was quietly amused at being told things he already knew from his studies in Washington. He had no qualms about our children being brought up as Catholics. We were married in a Catholic church in Oxford, exchanging vows outside the sanctuary. Later that year we moved to New York. It was always important for Richard that I should grow in my faith and practise it diligently. I started going to Mass and Communion every morning. One day I wasn't fasting before Communion (as was the custom then) and Richard asked why. I told him I had decided I was going to have breakfast with him each morning. He said no, that I should go to Mass, which I did. And then he contracted Hodgkin's disease and died after a year into our marriage, just weeks before his twenty-eighth birthday. It was only a year of marriage but by then we had developed a recognised union, embraced by an infinitely loving God. As Richard had said in his poem 'The Coast', 'know that ... the one riddle, the one great enterprise in this world/is to learn how to love and keep loving'.

Before I met Richard, I was what could be called a routine Catholic. Richard brought my faith alive, made me examine it and commit myself fully to it. It was really a kind of conversion. Our love for each other deepened our rootedness in God. The great spiritual bond between us helped me to cope with his loss after a year's marriage. I was very consoled by the fact that Richard had baptism of desire (a phrase we rarely hear nowadays) before he died. He had expressed a wish to talk with a wise man, not necessarily a priest, and a mutual friend of ours arranged this. To me that was manna from heaven – deep, deep consolation.

His death was not in any way a blow to my faith. I don't understand that mindset that suggests I might have been angry with God. I know him to be an infinitely loving God and everything that happens is lovingly planned for us. God doesn't push or force us – ever. We have free will after all. On the night Richard died, I knew what I wanted to do for the rest of my life: get to heaven as quickly as possible and be with Richard. I would enter monastic life. This could not happen overnight. I would have to be tested and tried over a period of years until the Abbess and her council would decide to accept me. I wanted to be in a contemplative rather than an active order. I met a wonderful

Dominican theologian, Fr Anselm Moynihan, who guided me in my choice. I wanted to be incognito, with no publicity whatever. In the end I settled on Stanbrook, a Benedictine monastery in the British midlands. While I was searching for the right monastery, I continued working, and lots of work – television, records, a concert tour of Australia and New Zealand – came my way. So I kept on working but always with this other goal in mind. It was actually five years after Richard's death that I entered Stanbrook. I fitted in wonderfully there. They loved me and I loved them and I have kept in contact with them over the years. Father Anselm had told me that my charity tended to be vertical rather than horizontal, so the obligatory one hour's recreation each day when everybody had to talk among themselves helped me work on that particular flaw of mine. I was very contented there.

I don't see God as a 'person'. I believe in what was said to Julian of Norwich, the thirteenth-century mystic. Christ said to her, 'I am in you and you are lovingly enfolded in me.' That is what I have always held on to. We are baptised into Christ. We are one with him and any separating that is to be done will be on our part, not his. In Stanbrook I had come from an Ireland where religion had a sort of Good Friday orientation – dark and sombre. I entered in Easter week. I remember the Abbess giving a talk to the community about the joy of the resurrection. I was saying to myself, what's all this about joy? I went to the Novice Mistress who gave me books on the subject. The big, explosive book was *The Resurrection* by F. X. Durrwell, a French Redemptorist priest. This was a seminal book around that time. I saw Christianity in a new light – the cross transformed by the certainty and joy of the resurrection. I became hooked on theological reading, particularly Durrwell. To this day, I read anything of his that I can.

Despite my contentment at Stanbrook, where I was solemnly professed in 1967, my health deteriorated and when I became ill for the second time in a few years, the medical advice was that

I should consider leaving the monastic life. Having prayed and thought about it, and having discussed it with the Abbess and my close friends in the community, I decided to leave and return to the world. Eventually, I resumed my singing career, reluctantly, after an appearance on the *Late Late Show*.

My faith has always been central to my performing life. It is the real core of my life, and prayer is an indispensable part of that. I love the liturgy and find it extremely enriching. We have only Sunday Mass on Aran where I live now. When I come to Galway I make an effort at daily Mass – there are so many churches. When I don't have that, I read the liturgy for nourishment and, of course, I couldn't be without theology, especially Durrwell and Karl Rahner. I try to meditate but I don't find it easy. My mind wanders.

We are not alone. In one sense you and I are not in charge of this conversation. The Holy Spirit and Jesus are in on it. It is that Julian of Norwich thing again: 'I am in you.' I feel I have to love everyone I meet on the street, however repellent or criminal some of them might be – they are all Jesus. We have to live the faith, but we have enormous help in Jesus who is in all of us and who does the loving. From reading Durrwell, I understand the Spirit as the love between the Father and the Son and as being the power of God.

So much of what we believe is mystery, but that doesn't bother me. I know that I know next to nothing and I trust that I will be given the measure of understanding I need. I don't force myself. I find nourishment in theology. Father Anselm knew me inside out spiritually and I never questioned him whenever he gave me a book to read. Once he gave me another of Durrwell's books, *Mary: Icon of the Spirit, Icon of the Church*. I didn't say anything to him, but up to then I had never read a book on Mary that had made any impact whatsoever on me. I took it on holiday and when I began reading it I couldn't put it down. I learned more about the mystery of the Trinity from that book than from any book I ever read on the Trinity. As far as I'm concerned, nobody can beat Durrwell, whose writings are all scripture based.

In 1975 I met Pat O'Toole, who had returned seriously ill from Africa, where he had been a missionary and school headmaster. We became good friends and he helped me find my way back into the world of performing. Ultimately he became my manager and by 1985 we were in love. We were married in Canada, where I was on a concert tour. Pat has been a benign presence in my life. He is incredibly patient and resourceful and has a much more kindly attitude to everyone than I could ever have. We spent six wonderful years in East Africa where Pat was teaching. The joyousness of the faith in the people there was quite remarkable. Nobody trained them in singing, but they can almost literally raise the roof and they harmonise instinctively. And in the midst of great poverty the children were always happy.

I have a strong devotion to Mary. She is the mother of Jesus, our spiritual mother, and having been born in the month of May, she is my patron. She is my first ally when I pray that Pat will overcome the cancer he is struggling with. I have people all over the place praying for this one thing and Mary is spearheading the team! I think we don't ask our Heavenly Father for enough things. Jesus said, 'If you remain in me and my words remain in you, ask what you will and you will get it.' A priest friend explained 'My words remain in you' as living as Jesus lived, loving other people. That can be the difficulty for me – reminding myself that each person is Jesus and is infinitely loved. In some ways it is so wonderfully simple, but the living of it is a challenge.

I love silence. I have a beautiful quotation from the *Philokalia* [texts written over a thousand years ago by contemplative monks of the Eastern Orthodox tradition]: 'I see that you too have been wounded by the arrow of the love of silence.' I don't think my love of silence is necessarily due to my time in the monastery. It's innate in me. There is a silence which is part of music, threading its way through; as John Montague puts it, 'the delicate dance of silence'.[1] I loved the silences of Africa. I love 'nothing', when there is no noise around. Just to sit and be.

I think doubt accompanies faith. Every day we encounter doubts. I try to counteract them with acts of faith. I pray, 'Jesus, Son of God, have mercy on me.' Or I recall that wonderful quotation from the prophet Micah,'There is only one thing Yahweh asks of you, only this – to love tenderly, to act justly, and to walk humbly with your God.' That sums it all up for me.

Death will come to us all, but hopefully when it does we will be totally engrossed in God. I am indebted to my friend Fr Anselm for that most comforting thought. He once lent me the notes he had when giving retreats to contemplative orders. Jesus said, 'Whoever believes in me shall never see death.' Anselm explained the word 'see' as meaning 'to be aware of, to pay attention to'. On that basis, we cannot really fear death, so I am very heartened by those words. And there will be a wonderful afterlife. We cannot have any concept of what it is but as the great Karl Rahner says, 'Heaven is not a place or a state. It's a different order of being.' I understand that to mean that we haven't the equipment to conceive of it. A 'different order of being' will do for me. It's a leap of faith but then faith is all about leaping! There is so much we cannot grasp – for example, that there was no gap between Jesus dying on the cross and the ascension. I read this in an article by Sebastian Moore OSB, 'Notes Towards a Theology of the Redemption'. He argues that the 'gap' is merely an accommodation to our senses. God is not bound by time and space, unlike us. We are all in God's 'now', an infinitely loving now, as I often say to Pat when we discuss these things.

I am anchored in my belief and grateful. I came across another quotation in the *Tablet* magazine: 'The best thing you can do

---

1. John Montague, 'Woodtown Manor', *Selected Poems* (Toronto: Exile Editions, 1991), 34.

for yourself ever, no matter what happens to you, is to praise him and thank him.' I am grateful for the gifts that have been showered on me left, right and centre, and for the strength to cope with the not-so-good things. Nothing is random. I didn't choose to be a performer. My career chose me. In every concert, my focus was ultimately on God – that what I was about to do would enable my audience to know and love him better. There is an infinitely loving plan of his in everything. We need to trust in that.

MÍCHEÁL
Ó MUIRCHEARTAIGH

Mícheál Ó Muircheartaigh was born in Dún Síon, Co. Kerry. He was educated by the De la Salle Brothers in Ballyvourney, Co. Cork, and later at St Patrick's Training College, Dublin, from where he graduated as a primary teacher, and at University College Dublin. He taught for over thirty years, but it is as a radio commentator on Gaelic games that he won fame. In a broadcasting career of over sixty years he became 'the voice of Gaelic games', and his vivid and colourful commentaries, often laced with memorable quotes and anecdotes, won him legendary status. Now retired, he is much in demand as a speaker and charity commentator. His autobiography From Dún Síon to Croke Park *was published in 2004.*

I suppose faith is an acquired gift. You arrive into it. You become conscious of it. In my time and place, County Kerry in the 1930s, there was no other option but the Catholic faith. From very early in my life I heard God mentioned in the everyday language of the people. We spoke a lot of Irish, and when a neighbour called in at night, as he opened the door he would say, '*Bail ó Dhia anseo isteach*' (A blessing from God on all here) to which the reply was '*Go maire tú i bhfad*' (May you live long). It was a simple message of goodwill, but the mention of *Dia* was part of our culture. It was *fite fuaite* (interwoven) with every small thing. If someone sneezed, you said '*Dia linn!*' (God be with us). If you met someone in the street, you greeted them with '*Dia is Muire dhuit*' (God and Mary be with you) and they might reply, '*Dia is Muire dhuit is Pádraig*' (God, Mary and St Patrick be with you). The presence of God was all around you in the course of every day and you could not but be aware of it. It was very difficult to imagine him, but he resembled a being that was all-powerful, to whom nothing was impossible. Everything would be sorted *le cúnamh Dé* (with the help of God). This being could help any cause or any person. He had a power beyond belief.

I grew up in a faith-filled and prayer-filled home. The rosary was an accepted part of daily life, recited quickly or slowly depending on family commitments. *Coróin Mhuire* (Mary's Crown) we called it, and of course there was something special and powerful about Muire. She was *An Mhaighdean Bheannaithe* (the Blessed Virgin) who had been assumed into heaven, swept through on a fast track like first-class passengers in an airport, while the rest of us had to go the hard road, overcoming obstacles on the way, with no guarantee that St Peter might not deny you entrance to heaven at the last minute. 'Faith' was simply absorbed in the language, culture and everyday life of your community.

Once every five years we would have the stations in our house, for which there would be much painting, decoration and cleaning in advance. Two priests would come – the parish priest and the curate. One went 'up to the room' for confessions while the other said Mass for the assembled family and neighbours. Then they reversed roles – a second Mass and more confessions. During Mass the parish priest collected what we all referred to as 'oats money' – a tradition going back to the time when the priest came on horseback and feeding his horse was a big thing. There was one priest who was noted for saying, '*Tabhair punann don gcapall*' (give the horse a sheaf of oats), and maybe before the second Mass he would say, '*Tabhair punann eile dó*' (give him another sheaf). The head of the family gave the 'oats money' – what we learned in our catechism as 'contributing to the support of our pastors'. And all the time nobody queried any aspect of the faith. The commandments were there to be obeyed, and if you erred in any way confession on Saturday night was part of the weekly ritual. At school with First Holy Communion and the rote learning of catechism and its inspection, faith and God were very much imprinted on our young lives.

This continued at secondary school. I went to the De la Salle Brothers in Ballyvourney and we had Mass every morning. The approach of the curate's car from the village signalled the ringing of the bell for Mass, which each student served at in turn throughout the year. We had an annual retreat, with three days of total silence, during which the Redemptorist priests preached and wrought fear in our hearts with their sermons. The fear of God was so powerful. You were constantly reminded that if you strayed off the correct path, then the great power of God could be used against you. Again, nothing was queried. We all believed. We all practised our faith. Even later, at third level, when I went to St Patrick's Training College in Dublin, daily Mass was *de rigeur*. The dean went through the dormitory every morning, ringing his bell and proclaiming '*Benedicamus Dominum*' (Let us bless the Lord) outside every cubicle and waited for the response, '*Deo Gratias*' (Thanks be to God). If there was no reply he proclaimed in a louder voice until he got the required response. Nothing had changed in the practice of our religion.

The culture of fear was common at home also, especially at mission time. Purgatory and hell were leaned on heavily by the missioners who came to strengthen our wavering faith. No one doubted the missioners' sincerity, but they might not have needed to speak so hard at the people, often frightening grown adults with their fiery oratory. There were separate missions for men and women. Later, in my broadcasting life, myself and two colleagues were attending a football match in County Louth. The Saturday evening vigil Mass had just been established, and on enquiring, we were told there was a 7 p.m. Mass in Drogheda. We went along to a full church and, as was our wont, stood at the back with our arms folded. We noticed nothing unusual until a priest approached us and informed us we would have to leave. It was the closing of the women's mission and he duly absolved us of all obligation to attend Mass. They were different times.

Change did come when I entered the world of work as a teacher. There were ten of us young lads in digs in Dublin, representing all shades of belief and none. We even had a thoroughbred Communist from Mayo in our midst, who was always preaching at us, hoping we would 'see the light'. There were great debates and arguments on all sorts of topics. The Communist decided to get married and to do that he had to go to Confession. We brought him to Whitefriar Street church, where there was a famous priest known as 'Flash' Haughey. He got the nickname for the speed at which he went through confessions. The Mayo man was in and out in a flash and he was the happiest man in the world. Working in Dublin and studying for a degree at night, together with the company in digs, all made for a very broadening experience. Another point of view is never bad.

In Ballyvourney we had learned reams of poetry. We would recite them aloud and sometimes change them to suit our circumstances. A favourite one was *Comhairle na Bardscolóige dá Mhac* ('The Bard's Advice to His Son') which included the lines, '*Ná tabhair do bhreith ar an gcéad scéal/Go mbeirfidh an taobh eile ort* (Don't give a verdict on anything until you hear the other side, no matter what it might be). It's worth listening to; then make your judgement. In my own case, I listened but my judgement still came down on the side of the faith I had grown up with.

Faith can come to us in many ways. The late Kerry philosopher John Moriarty told a lovely story about his father. He had started life as a travelling farm labourer. He loved his work and he loved the land, harbouring a longing to own his own land some day. He went to America, saved up his money, came home and bought a farm in Moyvane. He always kept about twelve cows that were very special to him. 'Them cows adores me,' he would say. On the way home from the field they would go at their own pace, grazing along 'the long acre'. He would never disturb them, but waited for them to make their own way to the byre. He believed that was their heaven – to be warm and secure in their own place. He would smoke his last cigarette of the day with the cows before he went to bed. I can imagine them chewing the cud, as if agreeing with everything he said and thus making him happy. He had a great fear of death, however. Not knowing what to expect made him very anxious. John said to his father, 'You will have no problem. When you get up there, those cows will be waiting for you. They will know the way to another heaven. They will lead. You will follow.' The fear fell away from his father. He was a new man. That was his particular belief – that there was some special place for him to be happy. He was being led there, maybe by people as well as cows. I love that story.

For myself, I believe in an afterlife and in the prospect of heaven. I cannot know what it will be like but it is great to look forward to it. It has to be there for us. When I go out on these frosty nights and see the pattern of the stars across the sky I ask myself how did all that happen. There is no logical explanation, some superior being must have caused all of this – this all-powerful one, to whom nothing is impossible. Getting to that heaven of course means crossing the great divide from this life. Death doesn't bother me, because it is unavoidable and therefore there is no point in worrying about it. The footballer going out on the field doesn't know the result of the game, but we know the result of the Big Game we are playing in since birth. The end result is defeat for one part of you – physical death – so you learn to accept that and face the next part with confidence of victory there.

A while before my father died, I bought him a nice walking stick. In ancient Ireland, a walking stick was a very acceptable present, maybe to defend oneself. He looked at it and liked it but said, 'I won't use it, but make sure it goes in the coffin with me, so I can have it when I go on my walks beyond.' There is a belief that death is the freeing up of another spirit in you which walks and wanders when you go 'beyond'. And it would be nice to have a good stick for that! There is the hope that we will see our loved ones again. We don't know in what form. Will it be, as the poem puts it, *ag fás* (growing up), *faoi bhláth* (in bloom) or *ag meath* (in decline)? Hardly likely, I suppose. It is a mystery. We have to accept that it is beyond us, for now. Our faith is full of mystery. As children we struggled with the notion of the Trinity when the shamrock was produced to convince us, but I suppose it means that there is more than one aspect to this supreme being. More likely three features of the 'goodness' we believe in than three actual persons.

I don't believe there is a hell. It was part of the old belief-through-fear approach. If we believe that God is all-powerful and all-forgiving, it is very hard to visualise that there could be a hell for all eternity. Like limbo and purgatory, it is not spoken of so much nowadays. If we can aim for godliness, doing good and caring for others, then we are well on the way to the right result. We have the Ten Commandments to guide us to a better way for all, but what is in the commandments that is not in the Magna Carta or any charter that sets out the rights and responsibilities that people should have? The different religions have all of these and we should accept that. *Beatha dhuine a thoil* – what people think is best for them. When the Dalai Lama came here, he was warmly greeted. He preached nothing that would offend anyone, only goodness. Similarly with other religions. Who are we to criticise? Maybe someday we will all be one. Common ground for the common good.

My faith has remained constant over the years. Going to Mass is important to me. Many people don't go nowadays, but that doesn't mean they are not Christian. By their works shall ye know them. It boils down to goodness, having good principles and doing good for others. The people who inspire me are those who give example by the time and trouble they take with caring for the poor, the homeless, the marginalised. People like Peter McVerry, but he is only one of thousands throughout the world who follow the example of Jesus to be loving and forgiving. It isn't always easy. I am reminded of a famous Tipperary hurler. He was Tipperary to the backbone and could never see them losing. When they did lose he would grudgingly say to his opponent, 'Sure 'tis good for the game.' But after saying it a few times he remarked to a friend, 'Jesus, 'tis hard to say it!' Maybe we don't mean it fully all the time, but even the gesture is something.

I don't harbour any major doubts regarding my faith. It is not a case of 'It was good enough for our ancestors, so it's good enough for us', but simply that it has worked for two thousand years and the Church has survived, despite many failings and jolts to its status. Recovery from recent events, like child abuse, will come and hopefully a different and better Church will emerge. Women will empower the Church of the future. They are 'doers' more so than men. Also there are so many gifted laypeople who can do so much of the work of priests, if given the opportunity. Greater lay involvement will produce a flourishing Church. That is my belief. I could be wrong. I forecast a while back that Fermanagh would win an All-Ireland. They haven't done it yet, but they will, they will.

I am reasonably contented in my faith and am ready for 'the final', but of course I am hoping that is a long way off! One of the great messages the Church has always preached is that of hope. Hope is a wonderful piece of armour to have. If today is bad, tomorrow may not be and may be even better. *Bíonn cabhair Dé ar an mbóthar* (God's help is on the road), wherever you are. Or *Is gaire cabhair Dé ná an doras* (God's help is nearer than the door). You only have to ask.

MARY REDMOND

Mary Redmond was born in Dublin and educated at Loreto College, St Stephen's Green; University College Dublin and Cambridge University. She is a leading employment lawyer and an adviser and consultant on labour law and industrial relations. She has written extensively on these subjects, notably on dismissal law. She founded the Irish Hospice Foundation following the death of her father. She also founded The Wheel, a network of voluntary and social groups, and is chairperson of a wide range of boards in the commercial and voluntary sectors. Her own experience of cancer led her to compile The Pink Ribbon Path *in 2013, a book of prayers and reflections for women with cancer.*

I believe God exists. If I could describe him I would be in a unique category, because down the ages people have tried to describe the Holy Other, the Cloud of Unknowing, the No Thing. We are all religious beings. We have a hunger to understand the first cause and the final end of all things. We see in Buddhist texts, in the work of the Sufis, in the poetry of Rumi a search for life's meaning. As a great gift to us all, God has revealed his plans to us through the Word, and in sending us his son he has made known his plan for the world. Consequently, I believe in sacred scripture, through which I come into contact with the Triune God. Jesus appeared two thousand years ago and said, 'I am the Son of God.' That was either the most extraordinary deception or it was true and, as C. S. Lewis said, if there are no records supporting the former then we go for the latter.

Faith to me is a leap beyond your own reason. You make that leap because you know that the person who will catch you, loves you. It is following love into mystery. When you respond to that invitation to love, it is quite an extraordinary experience. When I read the gospels, I feel there is a universality in the word. It is the one word that all faiths are looking for, and that is an enormous gift. Someone has said that when you read the gospels, they actually read you. You get a living statement for your life at this time. The resurrection experience, so essential to Christianity, is as alive and relevant today as it ever was.

I grew up in a faith-filled house, blessed with fantastic parents. My father was a classical scholar who liked to translate Spanish mystics. He was chairman of the Revenue Commissioners, which might seem inconsistent, but there was a deep mystical side to him. He was active also in the St Vincent de Paul Society and the Catholic Social Service Conference. My mother had six children to look after, but she was also a member of the Third Order of St Francis. So I grew up in a happy Catholic family, where it wasn't just religion on our terms. I can remember my father talking about the love of the cross, with almost a tremor in his voice. He had obviously contemplated that at length. The priests of our parish were all supportive of our faith formation and I was educated by wonderful nuns at Loreto College, St Stephen's Green. We would go on retreats at school and we read a lot. I remember reading *That Man Is You* by a Belgian priest, Louis Evely. It was a classic work which made the gospels come alive. I also read *The Way* by Josemaría Escrivá, which was quite popular then and still is here and in England.

I went on to study law at college. The student years can be very difficult. You are moving into young adulthood and suddenly the previous safety nets are cut away. The values which you felt were secure are not necessarily those of the world around you. It is a tempestuous time, and if roots are not established you can very easily be toppled. At the same time we know we are supposed to become like children, which is a kind of a paradox; but only an adult can say, 'I want to become like a child.' I certainly had doubts at university. You tend to ask what the importance of all this is. Christianity is counter-cultural. You are in a culture where others act in a way that doesn't seem in accordance with what you are trying to nurture within yourself.

Paradoxically, doubts and difficulties can strengthen one's faith. Sometimes when Christ seems to hide his face, he is not actually hiding at all. In the darkness that you are experiencing, he is both hiding and holding you there. In some of these difficulties, if you just reach out almost with blind faith and say, 'It's over to you, Lord. I trust in you', you won't be let down. When God's plans are not your plans, it is very hard, but that is the time he reveals himself to you, when your own self-sufficiency is not there. I miscarried our first baby and then five years ago I was diagnosed with cancer – both very severe blows, but the self-sufficiency that I got in the True Self was enriching beyond words. Before that, losing my father was a huge blow. He spent a year in a coma following a massive brain haemorrhage, but I believe he was ministering all the time he was dying. That is why I started the Irish Hospice Foundation. Death is a major event in one's life. The hospice adds life to days by taking away the pain and allowing you to concentrate on your family and the next stage of your journey.

So much of what I believe is mystery and I accept that. When you take that leap of faith, you are going beyond reason. So many writers today use the prose of science and sociology – a prose that is completely incapable of describing the different tones of our lives and the feelings we know we have of things transcendent. There is no way I can describe the feelings I had when our son was born. It went beyond anything science could offer. When we make that leap of faith, the hands he extends are an invitation to love. The kingdom of God is about love. It's not the Church. It's not mystical experience. It's strong love and it has no distinctions, encompassing the entirety of humanity – Catholic, Buddhist, Hindu, Muslim, married, single, gay, straight. The message of Christianity is forgiveness and love. What is the point in having anger and resentment towards others? Of course there is mystery. If there wasn't, I would be equating myself with God.

Prayer is a big part of my life. All kinds of prayer – petitional prayers, loving prayers, prayers of praise. I am all in favour of 'shopping-list prayers' – asking the Father as a child, 'Please! Please! PLEASE!' As a mother I would prefer my child to say 'I want this' rather than 'If it's your will, I want it'. I think we are allowed to be children now and again! Some years ago, when I was ill, I was introduced to mindfulness meditation. I was somewhat reluctant at first but decided to give it a go, aided by my son who just happened to be president of the meditation society at university. I gradually became conscious of some sort of divinisation at work when I concentrated on my in-breath and my out-breath. I began to see mindfulness as something different and researched it on the internet. I found a chapter in a book on Christian contemplative prayer by a Carmelite priest, Ernest Larkin. He stated that Christian mindfulness very much completed the perfection of prayer, because as opposed to talking to God who is 'up there' – an intellectual concept – he suddenly found the immanence of God in the present moment. Larkin went on to write about Benedictines John Main and Laurence Freeman whom I grew to admire very much. It opened up a whole new world to me and I read widely about mindfulness.

I became aware of the World Community for Christian Meditation which was founded by John Main and I recommend it strongly. Christian meditation communities are monasteries without walls, where groups come together and meditate after listening to music or to John Main on audio. Personally, I spend thirty minutes in meditation, morning and evening. It becomes an intrinsic part of your life. You sit quietly, saying the mantra, *maranatha*, on the in-breath, and your mind grows quieter and quieter. It is literally seeing things with a new vision, introducing the newness of the gospels into your time and space. In peace, solitude and the absence of words, something changes in you.

You find yourself resting in the Lord, and who wouldn't want to do that? A friend of mine says that in meditation he inhales the Spirit in his in-breath. It is literally *inspirare*, breathing in the Spirit. Father John Sullivan, for whom I have huge admiration, said that without the Spirit we couldn't even say 'Jesus'.

My faith is completely central to my life and my work. It informs and imbues every aspect of my life for the better. My work and my life are not separate. There can be a great temptation to allow work to take over your life. Laurence Freeman described meditation as 'the wind in the sail of your soul'. If I want to experience that wind, I will turn off my phones, close my files, avoid the emails and make space for what is important. In the evening, I look over the events of the day, assess my behaviour, how it affected people, how I related to them. The community and voluntary sector is a very important part of my life – finding what can be done for the underprivileged, the poor (not necessarily in monetary terms), the marginalised. Life is like a three-legged stool – the legs being work, community and family. I am still on the path of trying to grow my faith, which I value more than I can possibly put in words. Doubts still persist. I can't always quell negative aspects of my ego, which may tempt me to go in different directions. Gandhi once said, 'I have so much to do today, I am going to have to meditate for two hours rather than one.' So yes, there are crosswinds, but I don't feel without help.

Faith is a gift for which I am exceedingly grateful. I give thanks that for some reason or other I listened to that invitation to love. Nothing that I did myself made me deserve it. I am also grateful for some of the bad things that have happened to me, because out of them has come good. The most supremely bad thing that ever happened was Jesus on the cross, and look what came out of that! I am grateful for all the insights and experiences I have gained and, above all, for the great gift of faith. That gift is there for everyone. So few people nowadays say, 'What does it mean to say I am a person?' People should be talking about that, the values they have, the importance of loving yourself and others as yourself. There is so much wisdom and so many reasons for hope in Christianity. Hope is equally a gift. I am a hopeful person. The family motto is *Nil Desperandum* (never despair). How could we not hope? Prayer is waiting in hope and in love.

I would love to have been with Jesus when he was lost and found again in the temple, because there are times when I have lost him and have followed the wrong path. Then I found Jesus and I said to myself, 'I won't lose him again.' This is an occasion of extraordinary blessing and gift and then there is the reaffirmation that you don't want to lose Jesus again. That's the symbolism of finding Jesus in the temple for me. He is there to be found by people who want to find him. His invitation comes to us when we are in our darkest moments. I have been in such situations regarding my health and personal matters. If you fall into bad health, I would go so far as to say that it is God's megaphone. He's calling, 'I am here for you.' And he was for me. I have tried to show this in my recent book *The Pink Ribbon Path*, authored in my married name, Mary Ussher (thepinkribbonpath.com).

There are wonderful examples of faith all around us in daily life. I was very touched by the faith of young Dónal Walsh from Tralee, who died of cancer. Likewise, the woman who went to the aid of Lee Rigby, the young soldier who was hacked to death in London: 'I did it because I thought that's what someone of my faith would do.' Everyone else was taking photos on phones but she acted, out of faith. Pope Francis is utterly inspiring to me. I love everything he is saying and I hope his example will be followed at every level. My parents obviously inspired me. I love the devotion to the rosary among Irish people – that to me is profound faith. I read people like Pagola, Main, Freeman, Bede Griffiths, Meister Eckhart – not for history or doctrine, but for nourishment. Magnificat is my daily companion.

We all wish death didn't exist but I think we have to look at it, think about it and try to lessen its sting. Every phase of our life is like a journey. I regard growing old not as getting over the hill but getting closer to the final stage of our journey. You spend your life looking and longing for God and now it's going to happen. The awful thing will be leaving the people you love behind. However, I pray that in the next life all the authentic good things I have known in this life will be there in the company of those I love, including those who have gone before me, signed with the seal of faith. I believe that. I don't know in what form we will meet but we will share happiness and the love of God.

Regarding heaven and hell, scripture says little enough. We are told that 'eye hath not seen nor ear heard, nor hath it entered into the heart of man what things God hath prepared for those that love him'. We can only try to imagine in a very limited way. It is interesting to read what saints like Mary Faustina and Catherine of Siena saw in their visions of heaven. Someone has described the desire for heaven as like a secret signature of a person's soul. The fire and brimstone notion of hell is metaphor. It has been said that if in life you sought separation from God and self-enslavement, that's exactly what you will have in hell. Going back to meditation, it helps to control negative aspects of the ego like ambition, power, money and being thought important. John Main described achieving that control as your 'dying' and finding your real self, so that when the day of our passing to the next life comes it is almost a second death. That puts things into a certain perspective.

In summary, 'My faith is my life and my life is my faith'. Faith brings you closer to the people you love, you love them even more. My faith encompasses everything I do and I am blessed that my husband understands this and is so supportive. Everything that I do in my life is encompassed in those eleven words.

ALICE TAYLOR

Alice Taylor was born in County Cork. She worked as a telephonist before moving to Inishannon in that county, where she ran a supermarket and post office for many years. As a writer, her memoir, To School Through the Fields: An Irish Country Childhood *(1988), was an immediate and unprecedented success. She wrote a number of sequels –* Quench the Lamp *(1990),* The Village *(1992),* Country Days *(1993),* An Irish Country Christmas *(1994),* The Parish *(2008) and* And Time Stood Still *(2012). She has also written three novels and three poetry collections. Her most recent publication is* The Gift of a Garden *(2013).*

I see God as the essence of goodness and my life is about striving towards that goal of simply being good. I think it is regrettable that we feel we must put a label on everything, so I am a little uneasy about 'defining' God. For me, life is about the balance of justice. If good does not balance the evil of the world or outweigh it, then we are all in dire trouble. I would see God as an influence to bring out the good in people, to behave well and honourably and not to wrong our fellow human beings or the environment. For me, God is a sort of ray of guiding light that attracts us to the goodness of life.

As children we saw God differently. He was the distant bearded father figure and everything in life was clear cut from the dos and don'ts of the catechism, which we learned off by heart. As you grow older the whole scene broadens out and becomes less understandable and more difficult to be specific about. In reality we are totally unable to comprehend God. Whatever is above us and beyond us is beyond human comprehension. So much of our belief is bound up in mystery. I accept that. I wouldn't attempt to grapple with the mystery of the Trinity, for example. I don't differentiate between the Three Persons. I wouldn't consciously think, this is the Father's job, this is the Spirit's job and so on. I would see them as the hub of goodness and I would see unity in them rather than separateness. We humans have a tendency to over-estimate our own importance – if we don't understand it, it isn't there or it's not worth talking about. In the heel of the hunt, does all that 'mystery' matter? What matters for me is the way we live, the way we treat our fellow beings, our sense of decency, our respect for others, ourselves and our environment. Keeping close to our spiritual side and nurturing it is the way to do that. Over the centuries the Church got bogged down too much with rules and regulations and forgot the inner self. As an institution, the Church became obsessed with power and control and that caused havoc.

For me, nature is the key to the creator and creation. Having grown up on a farm, I was very aware of how dependent we were on nature for the crops to succeed. My father understood the balance of nature very well. He always preached that if we wronged nature, we would pay a terrible price. I see nature as a huge sustainer of our spirit and sense of well-being. In my garden, working with the soil calms my inner being.

My belief in God is, I suppose, part of the culture I grew up in. We came from somewhere and I assume we are going someplace. I don't accept that because we don't understand something, it cannot be there. There is a presence beyond us, guiding us. I grew up in a faith-filled home. My mother was a very traditional Irish Catholic. Mass every Sunday, rosary every night. She practised as she preached. She had great belief in the goodness of human nature and saw people as maybe better than they were, whereas my father always saw them as they really were. They were a good blend, really. My mother was the praying woman while my father saw God in the fields. As I grow older, I lean more towards my father's interpretation of God.

In my teens and early adulthood, I didn't take my faith too seriously. I prayed when I needed to – at examination time, for example. It was the death of someone very close to me that really rattled my faith for the first time. Why should this happen, losing someone I loved so dearly? I was numb with grief and only went to the funeral at my sister's insistence. Again, I found the answers to my questions in the garden. It was a cold winter evening and everything had been pruned back. I thought to myself, it's just like me, cut back to the very bone. But spring will come and the garden will bloom again. Nature is a great healer.

I love silence. For the Eucharistic Congress in 2012 we held an all-night vigil in our parish church. It was very simply done. Different groups came at different times and silence was maintained all night – an amazing silence of people gathered together in prayer, meditation, writing songs in their heads, whatever. It was very powerful. Silence is a very scarce commodity in modern life. It's almost as if we are afraid of it. There's a tendency to fill silent spaces with music and noise. Silence removes the barriers to our internal reality. Are we nervous of being alone with ourselves? But being alone with ourselves is very calming. If I sit in my garden and watch and listen to the birds or watch the moon in the night sky, it is something magical. Yet this is only what is visible to us, and beyond that there is great wonder that we are not privy to. God is the conduit of our own inner goodness.

I pray each morning. We have Mass here two mornings a week and I go then. I like receiving the Eucharist. Again, I wouldn't get bogged down with the mystery of the real presence but the Eucharist enables me to think above and beyond where I am. I sit in silence and allow myself to 'be' within myself. On the non-Mass mornings we have a prayer service organised by eight teams of two. Every pair does it differently. I enjoy that. I have moved away from formal prayers. When I sit down now to pray it's more of a conversation. If you meet someone you know fairly well, you are hardly going to be sing-songing a set number of words at him. So I talk directly to God. Sometimes I ask him what he is up to. I talk/pray directly to the departed also. I ask them for different things and they come up trumps regularly! I feel more comfortable praying to them than to some obscure saint who lived hundreds of years ago. I like to meditate for twenty-thirty minutes each day. It is difficult but very worthwhile. John Main, who brought meditation from the eastern world, says it is very simple but not easy. I love his comparison of our minds to trees full of jumping, chattering monkeys. If we are calm, they are calm too.

The spiritual side of my being is very important to me. My mother always said we are not made of stone. There is another dimension to us and it is hugely important that we are aware of it and we look after it. Out of that comes our kindness and consideration for others. It takes us away from our materialistic impulses. If an alien landed on earth, he would be convinced that we are here forever, because we are so hell-bent on achieving everything while we are on this planet. Yes of course we need to achieve and accomplish, but not to the detriment of that other side of us.

I derive inspiration from books, music, art. I have been influenced by great spiritual writers like Anthony de Mello, John Main and John O'Donohue, but ultimately you evolve your own thinking and you mature. I find John O'Donohue's writings very inspirational. A CD of his on death was a great consolation to me after my husband's death. In bereavement you are in a terrible state, but John's beautiful imagery brought me into a new domain.

What upset me years ago, I would be more matter of fact about now. I have also grown more tolerant over the years. One of our greatest gifts is our creativity. I paint a bit and love to listen to music. When you look at a painting, there is a link established with someone who may have lived hundreds of years ago. I remember visiting the Musée d'Orsay in Paris at a time when I was feeling lonely after a death. I came across a painting of a small figure in the middle of a blizzard and I felt, that's me!

I felt such a connection with the artist. Any creative exercise is a step into our divine side. Creativity of any kind – baking, gardening, carpentry – is healing and links us with the divine. So it is hugely important to develop and nurture that well. We have a major drug problem in Ireland. I wonder if that is at least in part due to the frustration of people who have no outlet for their creativity. If I paint a picture, I get so immersed in it; so much that it becomes a kind of meditation. At that point there is no other world than that one. During periods of creative engagement, you step off the world into that little pool and it is so enriching.

As regards faith mentors, I was very influenced by my parents. My mother had a hard life, raising seven children on a hillside farm in north Cork. She worked very hard, but had a wonderful tranquillity and a great sense of values. She was very non-judgemental, which is a wonderful trait to have. I try to practise it in my own life and often find it very difficult. She enriched our lives with an appreciation of people and of the good things of life. I sometimes think she looked on us as the social services, sending us around to run errands for our neighbours or to look after my grandmother. She nurtured a caring nature in us. My father engendered a great appreciation of nature in us, even if we didn't appreciate it at the time. I have a cousin, Fr Denis O'Connor, who is a very saintly, unworldly, kind man. I am never impressed by people who say what *should* be done. I look rather at what they are doing. Father Denis is inspirational in that regard. There are so many people you meet in life who exude a certain well-being and goodness which enriches everyone around them.

Death can be tough. When my niece sang *Pie Jesu* (Andrew Lloyd Webber's Requiem, written to honour his father) at my husband's funeral, I understood how it captures the wrenching of the soul from the body. For some it may be just the closing of the eyes. For others, not so. I was with my aunt as she died. I was so aware that I was standing on the edge of a precipice facing into something so totally unknown. It is a mystery beyond our understanding. Despite all the advances of science, we are still behind a glass wall. I believe in an afterlife but I have no idea what it will be. I don't think we'll be resurrected in our own bodies – who would want that? There will be a shedding of all that and we will go on as spiritual beings. There is a little seed of that in us now, and that will take flight and live forever. You feel that 'seed' within you in prayer, in meditation, in silence. It nurtures a long-term contentment within you, preparing you for the next life. I trust in that.

If there isn't an afterlife, so what? We will have done our best and that makes a better world for all of us. It is important that we enjoy being here and make the most of that side of us that links with the eternal, hoping it will enrich us. There is a divine element in us and it's a constant struggle to keep it alive in the world we are living in. For me, wouldn't it be grand if heaven were a big garden! Imagine spending an eternity there. As for the alternative, I doubt if it is the hell we were taught about. I would wonder about the need for it, but there are evil people in the world. What will happen to them? I don't know, but the weakness of human nature saddens me. Whenever I go, wherever I will be going, I will have one question for God: 'Seeing how much suffering we inflict on one another in this world, why, when God made us, didn't he do a better job on us?' For me, heaven would be all that dry rot excavated out of us. I suppose it will all be clarified for us when we get there.

Ultimately, it boils down to belief and trust in a force greater than us that we just do not understand, like St Peter trying to walk on water. As long as he believed he could, he did! We are masters of our own destiny. We are over-institutionalised in the Church, which has evolved into something like a corporate business. There is far too much emphasis on structural hierarchies. We almost handed over responsibility for salvation to the institution of the Church when it was our own business, our own journey. I am enjoying my own journey despite several wallops along the way, such as losing my husband. But again what helped me greatly was the kindness of people. The greatest healer of all was and is my own creativity.

JOHN WATERS

John Waters was born in Castlerea, Co. Roscommon. His first venture into journalism was with Hot Press *magazine in 1981. He subsequently edited* In Dublin *and* Magill *and wrote a weekly column for the* Irish Times *for over two decades. He devised* The Whoseday Book, *which raised three million euro for the Irish Hospice Foundation. His many publications reflect his commentary on modern Irish society. They include* Jiving at the Crossroads: The Shock of the New in Haughey's Ireland *(1991),* An Intelligent Person's Guide to Modern Ireland *(1997),* Lapsed Agnostic *(2007),* Beyond Consolation: Or How We Became Too Clever for God ... and Our Own Good *(2010). He has also written plays for stage and radio and has entered songs for the Eurovision Song Contest. He is an ardent supporter of the Fathers' Rights movement.*

I am a Christian and for me that is a specific and concrete thing. I believe in a relationship that I have with the force that created me, for which the word Christ is apposite. I have no difficulty with that word and with the relationship I have with him. It comes down to having a different sense of my being to the one I might have picked up over the years as a journalist and writer, travelling about. This sense of Christ brings me to a different understanding of myself, which is of a being cast out here in time and space, on a journey. There are different dimensions to my existence which I can easily forget about, but which come awake in me when I start to go into this relationship with Christ.

I use the word 'Christ' rather than 'God' at this point in my life. As a child, I had a simple relationship with Christ. God the Father was a distant, austere figure. Then, as I described in my book *Lapsed Agnostic*, I drifted away from Christ to the world all through my twenties and thirties. I had a major problem with alcohol, which ultimately made me turn and look at myself in a different way and see something deeper going on. Much against my will, I began to reintroduce myself to concepts of God. At that point it was God the Father I spoke to. I never thought about Jesus for a long time. It took many years before I realised I was avoiding him. It was like when you fall out with a friend – you see him in the street but cannot bring yourself to acknowledge him.

I then met a number of Christians who weren't at all like Christians as I remembered them. When I was growing up there was an intensity about being a Christian that would have scared me. These people were intense, but in an entirely different way. They were intensely alive and intensely in touch with themselves and with the joy of living. That really attracted me. I wanted to find out where they were getting their energy from so I started to hang around with them. They belonged to an organisation known as Communion and Liberation. They were not in any way oppressive – they were just interested in me, in my life. So I started on this journey of relationship with Christ and gradually came around to be able to say the word 'Christ'. It reminds me of Václav Havel, the late Czech president and writer. When he wrote his *Letters to Olga* from prison, he never used the words God or Christ. Heinrich Böll, in reviewing the book, noted that Havel used terms like 'Beyond the Horizon', 'The Other', 'The Something Else' as if, out of courtesy to God, refusing to use the name that was being trampled underfoot by politicians. Christ was present in those letters. When I read the book again more recently, I could see it was very close to what had been happening to me in those troubled years.

As a child, I was a devout, pious little lad. My father always prayed alone, visibly, in front of the rest of us. I remember his prayer book, falling apart at the seams, stuffed with memoriam cards and leaflets. He never asked us to join in, and we didn't. My mother didn't pray in that way but went to church regularly. For several years I accompanied my father to the church for devotions of all kinds. Faith saturated the town. I have lovely memories of the Corpus Christi processions when there was an altar outside every door and the tar stuck to your knees when you knelt in prayer. I was a delicate child and missed a lot of school. As a result, my mother drilled the catechism into me for Confirmation. I arrived into school on the day the bishop was due to examine us in preparation for the sacrament. The brother grilled me for an hour, trying to catch me out, but mother had done her job well. For all that, I didn't really 'believe' anything – there was no need to believe things you knew to be true. Religion was central to everything. The whole town seemed to operate around the idea of God in a strange way. Christ was almost like your invisible brother. He walked around with you and you talked to him. He was present in your life. He protected you.

Then came the teenage years and I was seduced by the culture of the world. The piety of childhood had been attractive but the world of television and rock 'n' roll were attractive too. 'Freedom' was on offer. There was, it seemed, a choice to be made between Christ and the world, and I chose the world. For the best part of twenty years alcoholism took over my life. It wasn't necessarily wild living all the time. The freedom issue worked for quite a long time, but I felt I couldn't face Christ again. I felt he was untouchable. I was with Alcoholics Anonymous for fifteen years but ultimately I found their approach limiting – it stopped me growing spiritually. I was then lucky to meet people who helped me to see the big picture. I was brought around – despite my fighting it every inch of the way – to face facts about myself and to test the God hypothesis that I had rejected earlier. When I prayed, life got better and I was able to extricate myself from the anguish and turmoil that had descended upon me.

I came upon the work of Luigi Giussani, an Italian priest who founded an organisation called Communion and Liberation. He once said, 'Given a choice between salvation and freedom, I would choose freedom.' That made total sense to me. I had always been looking for 'freedom' but I simply misunderstood what freedom was. Ultimately, salvation can only come as a consequence of freedom. We can't protect ourselves from everything and achieve salvation. We have to take the risk of living, encounter doubt, temptations and seductions, learn about them and then find real freedom. In the past, there was a very strong notion in Irish Catholicism that the way to salvation was to stay away from the world as much as possible. I heard Pope Francis say recently in a homily that the Church is like a place where you stay in a room too long and the air is too stuffy. We need to get out in the air. There can be a risk in that but we have to take the chance.

When I fell off the horse and admitted I had a problem, I was lucky to have the time to ruminate and to meet the right people at the right time. When I stumbled across Communion and Liberation, I found it to be an extraordinary Christian movement. It has grown massively in South America and Africa but is still miniscule in Ireland. It comprises ordinary people, for whom Christianity is an axiomatic dimension of everyday life. For them, faith is a reasonable response to reality. Giussani takes you back to the moment of your birth. Using the intelligence you have now, what do you see? What do you feel? We feel astonishment and wonder at what moves, what is, and our place in the world. I now see myself in two realities. There is the journalist working here in Ireland in 2013 but there is also a kind of space traveller in me, coming through in a different way. It is an incredible journey, where I see everything so relevant and intensely real. I am still on the journey but at least I have a tentative sense of my existence as part of something far greater. And if you turn on the radio or television you might think what you hear or see is the whole of reality, but it ignores a whole other dimension of yourself. That is why I think faith seems implausible to many young people. They think science and technology have rumbled everything, but there is no real evidence for that.

There is an idea of 'faith' as something you go into church for, get down on your knees and grind your teeth until you 'believe' and then you go out to face the world. I think it's a different process: that of looking deeply into what is real and looking at people and their lives, seeing the mystery of where they came from and the extraordinary phenomenon that the human being is. People say to me, 'Why did Jesus come?' I'm here! You're here! Isn't that reason enough to start with? Consider that there are seven billion beings on this planet and you are one of them. This planet is a tiny speck going round a tiny star in a galaxy which is one of billions of galaxies in the universe. I am here now, a subjective consciousness looking out at reality. That's an amazing thing! Darwinism doesn't get to that level of understanding. The transcendent, the sacred and the holy are dismissed by many out of a desire not to be irrational. I have no problem with Darwin. He may explain everyone else but he doesn't explain *me*. As Giussani said, faith is knowledge.

Christ is the word I use for God, but for me that includes the Father and the Spirit. There is just the One. As a child, I saw Christ as a visible figure with a beard and a flowing robe, but now I think of him as the Spirit. He is in me. A lot of the problem in discussing these things is that words often block understanding as much as they help us. Words only take us a part of the way. Patrick Kavanagh understood that. The words were not the vital thing in a poem. It was the 'flash', as he called it. Kavanagh has been an influence on me from a long way back. He used to call himself a Catholic poet. By that he didn't mean that he was a daily communicant. When he saw the tree or the clod of earth, he saw the created thing and became acutely aware of his own createdness. That, fundamentally, is the alcohol story with me. I had moved away from harmony with Christ in search of the world and went with a different version of myself. The spine of myself became twisted, as it were, because what I was doing was not true. Once I came back into harmony and recognised

Christ as immediately present, things went a lot more smoothly. Kavanagh had that sense of the harmony of the created world which I found attractive.

As I interpret Giussani, the things we are taught as children are vital on our journey. In my own case I had rejected those childhood things as having no relevance to a growing man in a modern culture, but having fallen off the cliff, I found they were the most vital things I needed for my recovery. Things like the very idea of God and of my own self as a created, dependent being. I had baulked at the idea of being subservient, or in adoration of anything, but then to come on the idea of dependence – this willingness to kneel was the most truthful thing. There was no self-abasement in that, rather a great empowerment. That was the central element of my recovery, that what I needed for freedom was not independence but dependence on God the Creator, whatever it was that made me, because I didn't make myself.

I assume there is an afterlife but I don't necessarily focus on these things. I am on a journey, moving towards a horizon. Christ is showing me the way on that journey – how to live fully, how to deal with the world morally and ethically, how to take joy in every moment despite slipping off the ladder regularly. Doubt is ever present on that journey. One of the great damages inflicted on Irish culture was the sense that if you had a doubt, you were gone. Doubting Thomas would be a patron saint for me, because he demanded evidence. To know that there is a horizon we are moving towards, that is the way to live. What is beyond the horizon? There is something, but I don't know what it is. We can get mixed up with transcendent ideas that there is a house where the Holy Family lives and we are going to move in with them. Pope Benedict described the notion of eternity as the elongation of the present moment as an absurdity. Maybe it's a perfect moment that does not end. I don't know any more than that it is a possibility. We are on a journey and we should be prepared for everything.

Death doesn't bother me. I think that when death affects us so badly when others die, we project those feelings on the idea of our own death. No matter what you believe, death cannot be like that. If you believe nothing, what can death be but going to sleep? I don't take hell too literally. We can bring it on ourselves in this life. I went through it myself a couple of times, but beyond that I don't know. I once engaged in a series of debates with Peter Aitken, an atheist. We got on well together. Afterwards I said to him, 'Of the two of us, I'm the only one who has a chance of being vindicated. If I am right, both of us will know. If you are right, neither of us will know.' Peter replied, 'It's much worse from my point of view. If you are right, I am going to be very happy!' That defines where we all are.

I think that the functionality of a culture depends on the accessibility of hope. I am a hopeful person in the sense that the desire of human beings can only be buried for so long under falseness. That was my own story. You cannot live a life and avoid those questions. That for me is encouraging in a perverse way. I am a fan of Pope Francis. I was sceptical at first, but I see now that he speaks out of his own real experience. He will challenge us. I was in St Peter's last week [May 2013] and the gospel on Sunday was from John chapter 17: 'Father, may they be one in us, as you are in me and I am in you, so that the world may believe it was you who sent me ... that they may be one as we are one.' Those words are so central to my own journey. Christ is the centre of my being in the world.

JOAN WILSON

Joan Wilson was born in County Fermanagh. She was educated at the Collegiate School, Enniskillen, and Stranmillis Training College, Belfast, from which she graduated as a music teacher. She married Gordon Wilson, who had a drapery shop in Enniskillen. Their lives were changed forever when their daughter Marie was one of the victims of the Enniskillen bomb in 1987. Further tragedy came her way with the death of her son, Peter, in a car accident and the loss of Gordon from a heart attack. A woman of great resilience, built on a foundation of deep faith, she continued her music teaching career, which gave her great solace. With Alf McCreary, she co-wrote All Shall Be Well, *a bereavement anthology and companion (2008).*

I believe in God, the creator and the sustainer of the universe. I worship him and the Lord Jesus, Saviour and Lord of the world and I worship the Holy Spirit, the sanctifier of the people of God. I worship the holy, blessed and glorious Trinity, because there is no other where to go. Jesus once asked Peter did he believe in him and Peter said he did, because where else would he go. That is my feeling also.

The origin of my belief is learning the Lord's Prayer at my mother's knee and many more prayers besides. I loved the simple little hymns: 'Jesus, Tender Shepherd, Hear Me', 'Hushed Was the Evening Hymn', 'All Things Bright and Beautiful'. My father wasn't a very religious man. He suffered greatly in the First World War and lost a leg in the battle of Cambrai. He later studied and taught music and started brass bands all over the country. I was an only child and when I was seven he bought a little violin, put it under my chin and wouldn't let me put it down until I could play a wee hymn, 'Jesus, High in Glory'. That was the beginning of my own musical career. My father had no time for the Catholic–Protestant divide. He used to say that when the shells were screaming over their heads in the trenches, they knelt down, Catholics and Protestants together. They were all in the same boat.

In our little elementary school of twenty-four pupils, the teacher told us Bible stories from the Old and New Testaments. I loved those stories. I remember at Easter she told us about the release of Barabbas. I was bothered about that for years, wondering in my little heart how the people could choose to free the robber Barabbas and crucify the good man Jesus. I then went to the Collegiate Grammar School in Enniskillen and hated it initially, but my father said I was there to stay and to make the most of it. Our maths teacher was extremely cross but she also taught scripture and taught it very well. She opened up the New Testament to us in a new way, and she presented us with the possibility to choose to follow the Lord or go the other way. I thought about that for a long time and went to a youth mission in the Presbyterian Church where the preacher outlined the choices before us. I chose to follow the Lord. I remember a hymn going through my head: 'Pass me not, o gentle Saviour,/ Hear my humble cry.'

On the way home my mother said to me, 'I'm very glad you made that decision tonight.' I suppose that was the beginning of my life with the Lord. I always wanted to follow the right path, which is difficult to do. I went on to Stranmillis Training College to become a music teacher. I joined the Christian Union there and had the opportunity to attend University Road Methodist church. The minister, Rev. Richard Morris, and his wife took great interest in us and brought us to a Sunday half-hour after the evening service, where we met the students from Queen's University and nurses from the Royal Victoria Hospital. They were lovely occasions. I remember too attending a Methodist conference in Grosvenor Hall where I heard a wonderful orator, a Dr William Sangster from London. He was known as a man of grace. He was ordaining students on that occasion and told them that when people came for Communion to them and stretched out their hands, to remember that those were the hands bringing their joys, sorrows, fears and anxieties to them and the hands that were toiling to keep them serving. He was the finest orator I have ever heard.

When I met Gordon we were both compatible in terms of faith. We both had a strong faith. We were both Methodists. I wasn't aware so much of the hymns of John and Charles Wesley, but Gordon introduced me to so many of them. They are so wonderfully written and are so much part of my life. I love singing them – 'Love Divine, All Loves Excelling', 'Oh For a Thousand Tongues to Sing', 'A Charge to Keep I Have':

> A charge to keep I have
> A God to glorify
> A never-dying soul to save
> And fit it for the sky.

They are part of my prayer-life, of how I express my belief. A favourite of Gordon's was 'Jesu, Lover of My Soul':

> Other refuge have I none,
> Hangs my helpless soul on Thee;
> Leave, ah leave me not alone,
> Still support and comfort me.
> All my trust in Thee is stayed,
> All my help from Thee I bring;
> Cover my defenceless head
> With the shadow of Thy wing.

These hymns, and those of Isaac Watts and Mrs Cecil Frances Alexander, are ideal for family occasions – weddings, funerals, etc. For our wedding, we chose 'Love Divine' by Charles Wesley:

> Love divine, all loves excelling,
> Joy of heaven, to earth come down,
> Fix in us thy humble dwelling,
> All Thy faithful mercies crown!
> Jesu, thou art all compassion,
> Pure unbounded love thou art;
> Visit us with thy salvation!
> Enter every trembling heart.

And then the final verse:

> Finish then thy new creation,
> Pure and spotless let us be;
> Let us see thy great salvation
> Perfectly restored in thee;
> Change from glory into glory,
> Till in heaven we take our place,
> Till we cast our crimes before thee,
> Lost in wonder, love and praise.

Those words so encapsulate our belief, our joy in the Lord and our aspirations. And the theme is love, which we further underlined in our choice of reading, the Song of Love from Corinthians 1:13.

Life experience has strengthened my belief over the years. Putting my trust in the Lord, no matter what comes. I pray daily for my only remaining child, Julie Ann, and her family; for Peter's family; for the sick; for peace in the world; for people who still write to me since Marie's death. Prayers of thanks are also so important. A minister friend of mine used to say, 'When we go to heaven, we will be sorry we did not pray more.' Listening to good preaching affirms my faith, as does daily Bible reading. I have been a member of the Scripture Union since I was fourteen and use their excellent notes and guides when studying the Bible. I like to read Christian books, especially those of John Stott, former rector of All Souls Church, London. His *Through the Bible, Through the Year: Daily Reflections from Genesis to Revelation* is a favourite of mine. Doctor Leslie Weatherhead, who was a great preacher in London, compiled a book, *A Private House of Prayer*, which offers comments, Bible readings and meditations for daily use. It's a great old book and I keep going back to it for strength and comfort. I used to pray for specific things, but in recent years I just pray that God's will be done in all things. Probably the greatest source of strength and grace is the great privilege of going to the Lord's table for Holy Communion. Think of the Last Supper. When Jesus celebrated with his disciples he gave a new meaning of God's redemptive power with the words, 'Do this in memory of me.' A simple sentence that started in the upper room and continues the celebration throughout history and throughout the world. We thank God at his table for the wonderful opportunity to ask for his forgiveness and to grant us a new beginning.

I have had three great losses in my life – Marie in the bombing, our son Peter in a road accident and Gordon from a heart attack – and I needed all the strength and grace God could give me, which he did, but it was very hard. I was very angry with those who killed Marie. We were inundated with media, and I was shattered for days. I couldn't have got through all of that if God wasn't with us every minute of every day. Gordon's words were typical of him, but I was going to need time. I had no anger with God. I thank God that Marie knew the Lord. She used to go to lovely services in Belfast and made several comments about them in her diary, and also little prayers asking God to guide her in her work in the hospital. Peter's death was unbelievable. Gordon and I felt we must do all we could to support his wife, Ingrid, but within six months Gordon was taken. It was a very hard blow. I was very lonely. It was a day-to-day struggle but I often said to people, 'God's timing is best.' He knows. He will sustain us. Gordon always said we would get the grace to carry on, and we did. I still need God's grace because I can be very volatile.

I have lived on my own for eighteen years. Time is not the great healer. It helps you accommodate but the wounds are still there and can be reopened. Listening to Handel's *Messiah* is a great comfort. 'I know that my Redeemer liveth' gives me a great lift. The resurrection was the greatest thing that ever happened. God raised Christ from the dead and set his seal on the atoning work. Music generally is a great source of comfort to me. The Priests were here for the G8 Conference and when they sang 'Lift Thine Eyes' from Mendelssohn's *Elijah*, it filled me with joy, peace and thanksgiving. Recently we had the Ulster Orchestra here with a soloist who played Mozart's *Violin Concerto in G*. That healed me, gave me energy, sent me out a new person.

I believe in the afterlife. I have tried to read Revelation but it is a very difficult book! I think we shall see Jesus face to face. As it says in *Messiah*, 'In my flesh shall I see God.' I think we will see our loved ones as we knew them. Saint Paul says we will know each other. It is a mystery to us now of course, but in the twinkling of an eye it will all happen. A place of praise with no sin and no sorrow. The apostles, the martyrs, the prophets will be there. All will be revealed. All shall be well. We are imperfect now. Our finite minds cannot understand these mysteries now but one day we will be made perfect. Just leave it to the Lord because he does everything so well. It will be wonderful.

I think a lot about my own death but the Lord will call me when the time is right. I pray that I will use the time left as best I can. I want to meet the Lord first and he will lead me to my loved ones. It will be wonderful to meet David, whose psalms I love, and Peter, my favourite disciple. He was a bit volatile like me, whereas Gordon would say, 'Steady! Let's think about it!' And of course I never got to say goodbye to Marie, Peter or Gordon, but now ...

My faith is often beset by doubts. Why should God bother with an insignificant person like me? I can feel so careless at times, so useless. I can be selfish and try to please myself a lot. I cry for mercy and have to start all over again. I met a lovely lady from Cork in Tenerife once. She had had a lot of troubles in her life but every day she would say, 'I'm away to a chapel now, for I need mercy.' She was so right. And then there are the great comforting words from John 3:16: 'For God so loved the world that he gave his only Son, so that everyone who believes in him might not perish but might have eternal life'. All will be well.

If I could have lived in the time of Jesus, I would love to have been present at the Sermon on the Mount. Jesus had come from healing the sick and casting out demons and crowds had gathered, so he began teaching. He gave the crowd those wonderful guidelines for living, the beatitudes: 'Blessed are the meek, for they will inherit the earth ... Blessed are the pure of heart, for they shall see God (I think of the little children all over the world who have died) ... Blessed are they who mourn, for they shall be comforted (and, in my case, he did comfort) ... Rejoice and be glad for your reward will be great in heaven.' What a momentous occasion it must have been, but none of this is easy, of course. After Marie's death, I was in despair. I thought I would never be able to cope, but I came across these words of St Peter just eleven days after her death:

> Dear friends, do not be surprised at the painful trial you are suffering as though something strange were happening to you, but rejoice that you participate in the sufferings of Christ, so that you may be overjoyed when his glory is revealed. (1Pt, 12)

I feel I was guided to those words and they just carried me on. Any time I get down ever since, they come to me, because as Christians we can't expect everything to be perfect and lovely in this life. One day all will be reconciled in God's time, power and love.

Here, O my Lord, I see thee face to face;
Here would I touch and handle things unseen;
Here grasp with firmer hand the eternal grace,
And all my weariness upon thee lean. (Horatius Bonar)

JOHN QUINN

It is no easy thing to commit yourself to giving a 'personal testimony of faith'. It requires courage, honesty, openness and a fair degree of self-examination. It was easy for me to come up with the idea but it was only when I interviewed the twenty contributors to this book that I realised how much I was imposing on them, even intruding into their private lives. I therefore resolved to put myself to the same test by interviewing myself. The reader will judge the outcome, but I tried to be courageous, honest, open ...

The God I believe in is a long way removed from the God of my childhood. I don't see him as a person, but as a presence, a great power, almighty – so far removed from me, tiny little me on this tiny speck of a planet. It is so hard to comprehend, but I believe in him and that he created the world I live in. I can't prove it but I can see the wonders of that world all about me – the wonder of the human being, of the human mind which we still don't fully grasp in all its intelligence, creativity and wisdom; the wonder of nature, of growth, the whole cycle and order of life; the wonders of the universe way beyond this little planet of ours.

Despite the ingenuity of man and the wonders of technology and exploration, so much (how much?) is still beyond our ken. The most distant object discovered to date is about 13 billion light years away. How do you begin to comprehend that? And then what? We know so little, but still this wonderful universe could only have been created by an omnipotent power and for me that power is God. I have life from that power and I am unique to that power. I am totally in awe of that power and I am totally grateful to that power. It is a power that is ultimately beyond knowing, but I firmly believe in that power, that being, that presence, that is all about me every step I take every day of my life.

I was brought up in that tradition of belief. I had wonderful parents who handed on that belief to me. It was a very different world to the world when I became a parent myself, a much more accepting world. So much 'belief' was instilled by fear rather than by love or understanding. We learned our catechism off by heart (in my case not understanding the half of it) and were terrified of getting it wrong (especially when the bishop came calling at Confirmation time). We saw God as a severe judge who would condemn us to the most awful punishment for all eternity if we did wrong. The thing to do was keep the commandments and lead a good, God-fearing life. My parents lived that kind of life. My mother was a daily Mass-goer and said three rosaries every day for her children. My father was not as overtly religious but was a good and upright man. My Aunt Katie told me that as a young man he would go to the top of the brae near his Monaghan home on a Sunday after Mass with his prayer book to pray alone. It is a lovely image to have.

Like many of my time, I became an altar boy and served Mass and tried to be good. At boarding school, and even at third-level training college, every day began with Mass. That was the culture I grew up in. It was hard to avoid. There was no questioning or stepping out of line. We toed the line, which on reflection was not good, but at the same time faith is a gift which has been handed down from generation to generation. I am mindful of the hymn we once sang in Croke Park before matches: 'Faith of our fathers, living still, in spite of dungeon, fire and sword ...' Faith was obviously worth dying for, something worth protecting, something to be cherished. No small thing. So I hold on to that faith – not always an easy thing nor without doubts.

So much of our faith is bound up in mystery. We may be brilliant, intelligent beings, but we are still so limited in respect of knowing this power, this presence to whom we owe our existence. It is only natural to be doubtful, like Thomas in the Bible. We are curious beings and want to know the why of everything, which is good, but our knowing is limited. Mysteries like transubstantiation, the Trinity, the resurrection are hard to grasp, but there is a power in our uncertainty. For now we can only accept and trust. One day all will be revealed. For now, one can only express belief in the living of one's life. That might sound trite but it is no small thing to try to be good, to be kind, understanding, patient, loving towards our fellow humans, especially those who are not easily loved. To be helpful, concerned, to share what I have with those who have less are my aspirations, and I do try.

I also express my belief as a Catholic by partaking in the Eucharist. I always had a great affection for the Mass as a means of bringing me close to the God who made me. A day with Mass is a good day – a God day – when the community comes together to offer worship, thanksgiving, prayer and appeasement to that God. It has become, especially in retirement, a daily 'habit', but one worth cultivating, I feel. Together with the sacrament of the Eucharist – receiving the food and nourishment for our journey 'home' – it is a way of staying close to God. One could be cynical or extremely doubtful about receiving the 'body of Christ', but again it is a mystery and the belief, the reverence and the gratitude are there. The living of a life also involves trying to remain aware of the things that really matter. On all sides we are assailed by influences that try and persuade us that the here and now is all-important, that we must spend and consume and 'have' – that all this is 'good'. But is it? Is it really? This is a brief journey we are on and we have only one stab at it. If we maintain that material, selfish approach, we are not doing very well.

Prayer is an important part of my life. I have cultivated little habits over the years. On waking I reach for the little crucifix and dedicate the day and the protection of my loved ones to the Sacred Heart, with an added mention for the sick, the broken and the broken-hearted. If I get out for a walk I might manage a few decades of the rosary for the ill, the deceased, those with a cross to bear – not in any Holy Joe way, just as a way of using the walk well. I know Jesus himself taught us how to pray, with all the required elements – acknowledgement, worship, petition and appeasement – but my favourite prayer has to be that of John Henry Newman:

> May the Lord support us all the day long, till the shadows lengthen and the evening comes, and the busy world is hushed, the fever of life is over and our work is done. Then in his mercy, may he give us a safe refuge and a holy rest, and peace at the last. Amen.

There is such warmth, assurance and affirmation in those words.

I am hopeless at meditation. I am amazed at people who can do a 'Holy Hour' or spend a long period at exposition of the Blessed Sacrament. I would be gone in minutes, totally distracted by an over-active mind. For all that, stillness is important to me – just to take time out from the bustle of daily life – and I like to pop into the church at the quiet times, ideally for a chat, but invariably it becomes a 'shopping list' for loved ones. Formal prayer is only one kind of prayer, of course. So many people bear great crosses, make great sacrifices in life. I think especially of the disabled, the seriously ill, the parents, especially the mothers, of severely disabled children, for whom every hour of every day is a relentless struggle. That to me is tremendous prayer, far more powerful than I could ever aspire to. The philosopher Meister Eckhart once said, 'If the only prayer you say in your life is "Thank You", that would be enough.' I feel it is so important to give thanks to the Lord for all we are, all we have, all we hope to be. So last thing at night, I reflect on five things to be thankful for – simple things like a phone call from one of my children, a book or music I enjoyed, a comfortable home, a page or two of writing. There is never shortage of subjects.

Practice might not make perfect but it does strengthen one's faith. Likewise, the example of others: my parents; the ordinary people who live extraordinary lives, serving their community; missionaries and volunteers who work unsung with the poorest of the poor, the lost, starving and broken of the world in the slums of Brazil, Haiti, Africa. There are people I was privileged to meet in my broadcasting career, like Gordon Wilson, for whom 'the bottom line was love', or Jean Vanier, the founder of L'Arche, who gave up a comfortable life and career to reach out to the broken, lost and disabled. Their example could only strengthen my faith and make me realise how puny my own efforts are. Reading can help also. I am not a great reader of scripture, but I love the Psalms. They are so relevant, prayerful and so beautifully written. Like Psalm 138: 'I thank you for the wonder of my being, and for the wonders of all your creation.' Patrick Kavanagh's poetry is so spiritual, as in 'Ploughman':

> Tranquillity walks with me
> And no care.
> O, the quiet ecstasy
> Like a prayer.[1]

And that's the whole point. The ploughman prays as he turns the sod. The footballer, the artist, the musician – all are praying by using their God-given gifts. God is present in a Heaney sonnet, a Steinbeck novel, a Beethoven sonata – but we are all artists, in that we live out our lives as best we can, realising the amazing possibilities that lie within each and every one of us.

If I could have accompanied Jesus for one day on earth it would have to be for the Sermon on the Mount. What an occasion! Huge crowds clamouring to hear and be healed. And then Jesus comes out with the complete template for living our lives in the

---

1. Patrick Kavanagh, 'Ploughman', *Collected Poems*, Antoinette Quinn, ed. (London: Allen Lane, 2004), p. 7.

beatitudes: 'Blessed are the pure in heart, for they shall see God ... Blessed are you who are poor, for the kingdom of God is yours ...' But that wasn't all. He went on to chastise the rich and the false. And he went further: 'Love your enemies ... do good to those who hate you ... forgive and you will be forgiven ... Why do you notice the splinter in your brother's eye but do not perceive the wooden beam in your own?' What an extraordinary day it must have been! If it happened now, the TV cameras and reporters would descend from all over the world to send out rolling news about what this amazing man has said. An unforgettable day. And it's all here in Chapter 6 of St Luke's Gospel. (Memo to self: read the scriptures more!)

Timor mortis conturbat me – the fear of death disturbs me. When you get into your eighth decade, it is not unnatural to worry about the how, the when, the where of death. I realise I have no say in it, but just hope it won't be too painful or prolonged and that I will be ready. I have just been reading Isabel Allende's book *Paula*, the story of her life interwoven with that of her daughter Paula's coma and ultimate death. The last chapter is very affecting and beautiful as she accompanies Paula through the last hours of life. I have had my own experience of loss when my wife Olive died suddenly in 2001. It was traumatic and numbing and I still miss her, but I can only believe that she went on to a greater life, the *real* life. Therein lies more mystery – what is the afterlife, how will it be? A banner in our church proclaims 'In eternity everything is only beginning'. We just don't know. Will we meet again? I certainly hope so and will cause some trouble in paradise if we don't! It saddens me in a way that I won't see Olive again in all her physical, earthly beauty as I can't see how, logistically, we will all be reincarnated as ourselves again, but I presume her spiritual presence will transcend that earthly beauty. We will know each other as spiritual beings and be happy for eternity. Back to the scriptures again: 'Eye hath not seen nor ear heard, nor hath it entered into the heart of man what things

God hath prepared for those that love him.' We have to accept that. It is difficult to grasp but trust ... trust ... trust. All will be well and all in the end is harvest. That is an essential tenet of my faith.

So we struggle on. As St Paul said, 'I haven't yet won, but I am still running'. Words are my trade and the words of others sustain me. Words echo over the years from night prayers in boarding school:

> Christ before me,
> Christ behind me,
> Christ at my right hand,
> Christ at my left.

We keep going with the words of John McGahern:

> The best of life is lived quietly where nothing happens
> but our quiet journey through the day, where change is
> imperceptible and the precious life is everything.[2]

The hopefulness of the late John O'Donohue, who urges us to keep going

> Until this winter pilgrimage leads you
> Towards the gateway to spring.[3]

The lyrical beauty of the everyday so magically captured by Patrick Kavanagh:

> In the sow's rooting where the hen scratches,
> We dipped our fingers in the pockets of God.[4]

---

2. John McGahern, *All Will Be Well: A Memoir* (London: Faber and Faber, 2005), p. 360.

3. John O'Donohue, 'For Love in a Time of Conflict', *Benedictus: A Book of Blessings* (London: Bantam Press, 2007), p. 50.

4. Patrick Kavanagh, 'The Long Garden', *Collected Poems*, p. 43.

We keep going, with faith, hope and love, ever mindful of the words of the late and much-lamented Seamus Heaney:

> Believe that a further shore
> Is reachable from here.[5]

---

5. Seamus Heaney, *The Cure At Troy: A Version of Sophocles'* Philoctetes (London: Faber and Faber, 1990).